TALES AND LEGENDS OF THE
DEVIL

"How do you best the devil and live happily ever after? Read Claude and Corinne Lecouteux's *Tales and Legends of the Devil*, stories from across Europe, and find out. Claude Lecouteux is a master of unearthing hidden treasures from the European tradition."

ARTHUR VERSLUIS, AUTHOR OF *THE SECRET HISTORY
OF WESTERN SEXUAL MYSTICISM*

"Humanity's relationship to adversity personified and elucidated in stories teaches us the value of the cunning trickster. From either the vantage point of moral hygiene stories or the lack thereof, these stories show us the importance and folly of cunning, something we all need to be reminded of. Claude and Corinne have done a fabulous job."

MARCUS MCCOY, COFOUNDER OF THE VIRIDIS GENII
SYMPOSIUM AND ESOTERIC BLACKSMITH AT
TROLL CUNNING FORGE

"Claude Lecouteux has written extensively and meticulously on the supernatural figures that appear in what is often called 'the lower mythology' of the Middle Ages and has shown how these same figures (still) haunt our own world. More than twenty of Claude Lecouteux's books (including several coauthored by his wife, Corinne) have been translated and published by Inner Traditions over the past fifteen years. Why did I feel compelled to write a preface for this particular book? Perhaps because 'the devil made me do it.'"

JON E. GRAHAM, AWARD-WINNING
TRANSLATOR OF *THE BAVARIAN ILLUMINATI*

TALES AND LEGENDS OF THE
DEVIL

The Many Guises of
the Primal Shapeshifter

CLAUDE AND CORINNE LECOUTEUX

Translated by Jon E. Graham

Inner Traditions
Rochester, Vermont

Inner Traditions
One Park Street
Rochester, Vermont 05767
www.InnerTraditions.com

Originally published in French in 2021 under the title *Contes et légendes du diable*
by Éditions Imago, 7 rue Suger, 75006, Paris
First U.S. edition published in 2023 by Inner Traditions

Cataloging-in-Publication Data for this title is available from the Library of Congress

ISBN 978-1-64411-685-2 (print)
ISBN 978-1-64411-686-9 (ebook)

Printed and bound in China by Reliance Printing Co., Ltd

10   9   8   7   6   5   4   3   2   1

Text design and layout by Debbie Glogover
This book was typeset in Garamond Premier Pro with Zamora, Nocturne Serif,
and Gill Sans MT Pro used as display typefaces

To send correspondence to the author of this book, mail a first-class letter to the
author c/o Inner Traditions • Bear & Company, One Park Street, Rochester, VT
05767, and we will forward the communication.

CONTENTS

TRANSLATOR'S PREFACE

JON E. GRAHAM

In his long career Claude Lecouteux has written extensively and meticulously on the supernatural figures that appear in what is often called "the lower mythology" of the Middle Ages. His books not only free creatures such as fairies, werewolves, vampires, sprites, elves, dwarfs, and household spirits from the confused descriptions and misinterpretations offered by the learned culture of that time, consisting primarily of churchmen, but reveals their often hidden but tenacious links to the mentality of the pre-Christian world. By the same token, in accordance with the observation by medieval scholar Jacques Le Goff that "the Middle Ages never ended," Lecouteux has shown how these same figures haunt our own world, despite modern notions that dismiss them as delusions that our superior culture has outgrown. It seems more than fitting that, in this collection of tales and legends,* he gives his due to the

---

*As opposed to tales, legends imply the existence of an underlying historical reality that the stories contained in this collection would therefore rest upon. In the eras from which these tales and legends are drawn, few if any would contest the reality of the devil—circumstances that are hardly duplicated in our present post-enlightenment times.

figure the medieval church cited as the ruler of all these fantastic beings and spirits—the devil.

No one can seriously dispute the fact that our medieval ancestors fully believed in the devil. Opinion differs only as to the reason that this belief was so deeply rooted. Some suggest that what is now considered to be mere superstition was encouraged by the Church in the belief that fear of the devil was a stronger incentive than the love of Jesus for keeping their parishioners submissive to its will. But many of the most eminent scholars of these times, such as Erasmus, were equally convinced that the Prince of Darkness was a constant threat that required unsleeping vigilance, and the men of the church often secretly shared the beliefs of their flocks while publicly scoffing at them. Martin Luther may be the most prominent example, and the scatological nature of his recorded encounters with the fallen angel and his emissaries are well known.* Others have proposed that the devil may owe its persistent hold on the hearts of the peasantry to their persistent reverence for the ancient deities the Church transformed into devils to aid their efforts of conversion.

We don't find the devil of the theologians, nor the ambiguous, charismatic rebel that appears in the work of Milton and Hugo, in the stories that were part of a persistent oral tradition—one that could be still even be found in the more isolated areas of Europe well into the twentieth century (as can be seen in such books as *The Fairy-Faith in Celtic Countries* by W. Y. Evans-Wentz). The devil that haunts the fields we know is not the omnipotent figure described in the pulpits, that only unwavering conviction in the might of God and Jesus could turn aside. In this lower mythology he is more often a figure that must resort to guile to trick his victims

---

*For example, a bowdlerized version of an incident recorded by a colleague of Luther in Wittenberg describes the Father of the Reformation chasing off a devil by throwing an inkpot at it. In actuality this was a chamber pot, and in his flight the defeated demon left behind a foul stench that lingered in the room for several days.

into surrendering their souls to him in return for the wealth and leisure that are entirely foreign to the hardscrabble lives they led. To be honest, the price he offers for their souls seems like a bargain that most people of any era would have no hesitation in accepting. But the counter wager made by those who accept his offers in these tales and legends is that their own wit and cunning can upset the devil's plans and free them from paying the price he demands in return for three or seven years of a life of luxury, access to secrets forbidden to most mortals, or the love of a person whose affection they could never hope otherwise to gain. Those who can beat the devil at his own game often include blacksmiths, a figure that has been seen as a shaman and magic user since the days of Tubal Cain.* Another common protagonist is the third son or daughter that succeeds where their older siblings failed and ended up ensnared by the devil until freed by their often scorned younger sibling.†

Another common thread in all these tales—one that doesn't fall into the parameters established by the index of folk motifs‡—is

---

*Folklore, in fact, attributes the metallurgical arts to a blacksmith who tricked Old Nick into sharing his secrets of metallurgy and forging.

†In these stories, as in many other fairy tales, it is consistently the third or youngest child that prevails where their older siblings failed. I believe this may be because the oldest child was designated as the sole heir to the family's property and the next child was often destined for a life in the church. Having no future laid out like their older siblings, the third child was left to their own devices if they didn't want to spend the rest of their lives dependent on the charity of their older brothers in thankless toil on their estates. In order to succeed, they had to rely on their wits and know-how to think on their feet, hence their ability to sidestep the devil's snares into which their older siblings fell so easily.

‡Early folklore scholars studying tales and legends from different cultures discovered that they share many of the same motifs despite their chronological and/ or geographical remoteness from one another. This led to the effort to catalog these recurring motifs around the turn of the twentieth century. This index of folklore motifs was created in 1910 by Finnish folklorist Antti Aarne. Stith Thompson then translated it into English from German and expanded it. It was later revised and expanded again by German folklorist Hans-Jörg and is now known as the *Aarne Thompson–Uther Index* (ATU Index). In tandem with Thompson's *Motif-Index of Folk-Literature,* it is an invaluable tool for studying folklore.

that those best suited to beat the devil at his own game are not the high and mighty, but their modest and even penniless subjects. Time after time a king or wealthy merchant is forced to turn to an unassuming craftsman, soldier, or laborer to free the daughter whose hand he foolishly gave to the devil or to journey to hell in quest of something they desperately need.

We also learn that the devil is not a solo agent but has a family. A popular figure is the devil's grandmother, who will often protect the courteous visitor from her grandson's rampages but deliver the rude one into his claws. Here, too, the polite individual is often of humble status and the rude one someone of higher station, who discovered the source of someone's transition from rags to riches and tried to duplicate the actions that earned the poor man his wealth or rise in status. All this is greatly revealing of the mentality of the time, and shows that the people of this time could hold fast to ideas rooted in paganism despite the undeniable influence the Church had on their lives. The popularity and endurance of these tales testify to the resilient nature of these ideas, which can still be seen at work in modern cultural expression.

Despite what we may tell ourselves about the superiority of our modern world to that of our ancestors, the Middle Ages really hasn't ended, as medievalist Jacques Le Goff said. Not so long ago, musician Charlie Daniels recorded "The Devil Went Down to Georgia," a song about a devil looking for a soul to steal. Setting his sights on a fiddle player, he offered the musician a golden fiddle if he could beat him in a music competition. If the musician lost, he would not only keep his fiddle but gain the mortal musician's soul. Following a plot line that echoes many of these stories, the devil is bested and departs fiddle and soul free, irate and muttering under his breath about being bested by a mortal.

More than twenty of Claude Lecouteux's books (including several co-authored by his wife Corinne) have been translated and published by Inner Traditions over the past fifteen years but *Tales and*

Legends of the Devil is the first for which I've written a translator's preface. Why did I feel compelled to write one for this particular book? Perhaps "the devil made me do it."

JON E. GRAHAM is an award-winning translator, artist, and writer specializing in esoteric topics and surrealism. His most recent translation is *The Bavarian Illuminati* by René LeForestier, originally published in French in 1914.

Abbreviations of Works Cited

An asterisk indicates variants and counterparts
in other collections.

AaTh *The Types of the Folktale* by Antti Aarne

ATU Aarne, Antti, Thompson, Stith, *The Types of the Folktale,* Helsinki: Academia Scientium Fennica, 1961 (Folklore Fellows Communication, 184)

BP *Anmerkungen zu den Kinger- und Hausmärchen der Brüder Grimmer* by Johannes Bolte and Georg Polivka

CPF *Le Conte populaire français* by Paul Delarue and Marie-Louise Ténèze

EM *Enzyklopadie des Märchens*

KHM *Children's and Household Tales* by the Brothers Grimm

Mlex *Das Marchenlexikon* by Walter Scherf

Motif *Motif-Index of Folk-Literature* by Stith Thompson

TU *Index exemplorum* by Frederic C. Tubach

INTRODUCTION

Everyone thinks they know the devil, but how well do they really know him? The emblematic figure of evil who goes by the names of Satan and Lucifer and honorifics like the Prince of Evil or the Horned One is the demon that leads human beings to their ruin. Folk traditions quickly appropriated this emblematic figure and domesticated it to a certain extent, even stripping it of its terrifying aspect. This carries us a long way from the story of Doctor Faust and Mephistopheles.

This figure was embellished with traditional folktale motifs, which sometimes turned him into a stupid figure who could easily be hoodwinked and sometimes portrayed him to be as cunning as a fox. A variety of situations were used to bring him on stage, but mainly when it involved portraying him as a dupe or figure of ridicule.

The everyday lexicon has retained traces of the Evil One's omnipresence: people have a "devil of a time," a person signs a "pact with the devil," or sells their soul to him. People are now described as being a "real handful," but just a generation or two ago they were said to be "a real devil."* A person can be a "handsome devil," "a lucky devil," "a crafty devil," or "the devil's advocate," and we should not forget that "the devil can cite scripture for his own purposes." People can forget that "the devil is in the details" and

---

*This refers to medieval religious mysteries in which there were four devils.

1

then find themselves stuck between "the devil and the deep blue sea" when facing two undesirable situations; they will then "have the devil to pay." Other sayings remind us that "an idle mind is the devil's workshop" and "the devil we know is better than the one we don't," and if we "speak of the devil he is sure to appear."

It is said that the devil was handsome when he was young, that liars are the devil's children, that what comes from the devil will go back to him, and that the devil has twelve apostles. It is also said that wherever he doesn't wish to go he sends a priest or old woman, that he appears when invoked or when someone looks at themselves in a mirror, and that he left our world because he knows that humans are more than capable of cooking up their own hell. Some Germanic proverbs inform us that "devils only cry when nuns dance"* and that "men limp toward God but race to the devil." Meanwhile the French say that someone living hand to mouth is "pulling the devil by the tail," or the completely penniless

Mephistopheles appearing to Faust in his study, Delacroix (1828).

---

*Because dance was regarded as a sin by the Church.

person has the "devil living in her purse." This little summary is probably best stopped here as it could fill the remainder of the book and should be sufficient to show us how the Evil One is anchored in folk traditions.

What is unknown inspires fear, which is why the storytellers provided signs for identifying the devil: he is lame, as in Lesage (1707), has a tail or a horse's hoof, or even two, possesses one or two horns, has goose or pig feet, and a long nose.

> Two large horns could be seen at the top of his head; he had a bulging forehead, his nose was very long, and his mouth, which sat very low on a long pointed chin, had two sharp teeth. The belt of his voluminous frock coat was a horrible serpent opening its ferocious mouth. Muddy hooves stuck out from under his clothes, and his hands were clawed. He had a long tail hanging behind him that ended in a pointed arrow. He was black as coal, and a large dog baring its fangs accompanied him. This dog's tongue lolled out covered with slobber.[1]

Illustration by Nils Wiwel (1857–1914) for Ashjörnsen's story "Gutten og Fanden."

He appears in the guise of a hunter (of souls, of course), a dark man, a redhead, a priest, a woman, or an animal because he possessed the wonderful ability to transform himself.

It should be noted that the Vedic names for the devil are *kâmarûpa* or *viçvarûpa,* "he who changes his shape at will." We can see him as a handsome young man coming to fetch a fiancée, a dog, a black cat, a hare, a monkey, a black hen, a goat, a toad, a wolf, a bear, a horse, a dragon, a fly, a snake, and so on. Folk beliefs have cast the Prince of Darkness as the author of storms, hail, and thunder. This brings to mind the proverb: "The devil beats his wife and weds his daughter," which used to be said when it was raining and sunny at the same time. When it thunders, it is said that the devil is bowling.

Faust, Wagner, and the devil as a poodle,
Friedrich Gustav Schlick (1847–1850).

His hell can be visited, as seen in traveler's tales of the after-life, either because he hired a boy to be his furnace stoker or gate-keeper, for example, or because he abducted a human being. There are those who have apprenticed themselves to the devil, with the more daring signing a pact with him.

God's rival Lucifer played a role in the Creation, but *ad malam partem!** He created the wolf, the hare, the donkey, the goat, the wasp, the sea toad, and the skate. Plants also carry his mark, such as the *Succisa pratensis Moench,* which is known as "devil's-bit" or "devil's-bit Scabious." Other plants will send him fleeing. This is the case with mugwort (*Artemisia vulgaris*) and Saint John's wort (*hypericum*). He is the one that altered the juice of the vine and made it an intoxicating beverage.

His enemies are God and the saints, with Saint Peter hold-ing center stage as the adversary most capable of making him bite the dust. The saints James, Martin, and Bernard come into play in the Savoy region. In the medieval legend, Theophilus was saved by the Virgin Mary after he had signed a pact with Satan. . . .

According to another legend:

An enormous chain attached to a boulder bound the devil. He gnawed it all year long, and by Easter Eve all that remained was a sender wire. But on Easter morning, the Savior appeared and bound him with a new chain.[2]

What is especially striking in folk tales is that the devil has been entirely anthropomorphized. He is married, and one legend says this:

One day the devil took it into his head to take a wife, in order to propagate his race. He courted Impiety and after they wed,

---

*In a bad sense.

had seven daughters with her. When they had reached marriageable age, he desired for them to wed men in order to win their friendship. He gave the hand of his eldest daughter, Pride, to the powerful of the earth. . . . His second daughter, Avarice, he married to merchants and bankers. He gave his third child, Disloyalty, to farmers, mercenaries, and common men, and Hypocrisy to the priests who display a holiness they don't have. He gave Envy to artists, and Vanity was quite naturally the women's share. His only remaining daughter was Impurity. He pondered on to whom to give her, but after thinking on the matter, he decided to keep her at his home for anyone to come fetch her if he so desired. By taking this stance, he counted on having a large number of requests and visits, and his calculations were not wrong as experience has shown since that time.[3]

He has a daughter, a mother-in-law, a grandmother, a grandfather, and lackeys.* He lives in a castle or some other kind of splendid dwelling. When he lusts after a young woman, he adopts the appearance of an attractive man and woos the object of his affection, but he often imposes a taboo on her, which she, of course, breaks. His description is a far cry from that of Christian iconography in which he is hairy and has horns and clawed hands. Satan is also a skilled psychologist, and knows how to exploit human desires to his advantage—to one person he offers wealth, and to another love. It is interesting to note here that his preferred target is men. Did he fear the cunning of women who, in the tales, were sometimes able to hold him to halt or foil his designs?

The devil seems to like his peace and quiet, and would refuse entry to hell to any he thought were troublemakers. As for his rela-

---

*Their names are Goulu, Maquerel and Fremy, cf. Charles-Émilien Thuriet, *Traditions populaires de la Haute-Saône et du Jura* (Paris: Émile Chevalier, 1892), 520 *ff.*

tions with women, they are often comical. We laugh at the sight of Satan terrified by one of them; in fact, one woman terrifies him so much that he soils his pants. There is no lack of burlesque situations here, especially when the devil is given a good hiding or is conned and is sent fleeing with his tail between his legs.

The Evil One is not always ill-intentioned and sometimes does good, for example when he frees a prisoner or gives someone assistance.

Lastly, who is the devil of the folk tales? Comparison of texts shows that he is interchangeable with wizards or sorceresses, that he overlies fantastic beings that have been demoted from mythical status (such as the Lithuanian god Perkūnas and the woodland fairy or spirit Laume), and that "devil" is a term storytellers often use for the sake of convenience, a veritable portmanteau word. The marvelous is also represented by giants, objects—magic mirrors, purses that are never emptied—and magical fruits, transformations into objects or animals, a tree that is impossible to climb down from, and so forth. We even find an avatar of Chronos in "The Devil and the Fisherman's Daughters." And we can even see that the Evil One is mortal, as we are told in the story of the prince who enters Satan's service and frees the king of hell.

Our anthology covers twenty European countries. When a story is listed in Aarne and Thompson's index, we indicate the type of tale it is as well as its counterparts in other folktale anthologies, with the exception of the well-known collections of the Brothers Grimm.*

In some instances the reader will find two versions of the same story presented, separated, perhaps, by one or two centuries and location, but worthy of note because of the alteration of the

---

*We are not using any of the five tales from the Brothers Grimm that include hell or the devil: "The Devil with the Three Golden Hairs" (KHM 29); "Brother Merry" (KHM 81); "Gambling Hansel" (KHM 82); "The Devil's Sooty Brother" (KHM 100); or "The Devil and His Grandmother" (KHM 125).

essential elements, which thereby documents the evolution of the narrative based on the talent of the storyteller. Appendix 1 provides a tool to cross reference for these similar tales.

After a story, the section marked with the symbol 📖 provides some comparative sources and related literature concerning the tale or legend.

CHAPTER I

THE DEVIL AS SUITOR

1. How the Devil Recognized a Flea Skin

Bulgaria

A czar had imprisoned a flea inside a bottle and fed it for a good number of years. It grew, and once it reached the size of a calf the czar killed it, skinned it, and hung its skin from the front gate. He had a proclamation made throughout the land that whosoever could identify the origin of this skin would have his daughter's hand in marriage. When his subjects heard this, they all raced from all over to guess what it was—but none succeeded. One of them said, "It's a buffalo hide." Another said, "It's a calf." Another said this, and another said that, whatever crossed through their heads, but no one guessed correctly, so no one could wed the czar's daughter.

This was where things stood when a devil sprang out of the sea, changed into a man, visited the czar, and gave him the correct answer. He therefore won the hand of the princess, because the monarch could not go back on his word. The wedding took place at court, and then the devil left with his new bride to return to his domain. The czar accompanied them with a large retinue including some fife and drum corps. Walking hand in hand, the devil and his wife came to the shore and he dragged her with him into the sea where they vanished from the eyes of all. And now? Sorely distressed, the czar sent sailors in search of his daughter, but their quest was in vain. Most aggrieved and tearful, the czar did an about-face and forbid anyone to light a candle at night, celebrate a wedding, or sing a song anywhere in his entire kingdom. Heralds proclaimed throughout the land: "Woe to any who disobey this ukase!"*

An old woman who had six sons lived in the capital city. All were skilled, and each possessed a particular talent that was unique in all the world. Happy to be the mother of such children, the old woman lit a candle every night while singing joyful songs. When the czar's sergeants got wind of this they informed the czar, and he summoned her for questioning: "So, why have you not obeyed my command? You know full well that a merman carried away my daughter. Shouldn't you share my mourning and, with the fall of night, refrain from lighting a candle and singing?"

"Your Highness, so long as you and my sons, boys more valiant than any others, are alive, I have the right to do this."

"What is so special about your sons that you praise their merits so highly?"

"Know, your Highness, that my oldest boy can drink the entire sea in one gulp; the second can carry ten men on his shoulders and run like a three-year-old stag. My third son need only strike the earth with his fist to cause a tower to emerge from it; the fourth can shoot arrows higher than the sky and never misses his mark; the breath of my fifth son can bring back a dead man; and when my sixth son places his ear to the ground, he can hear everything that is said under the earth."

"These are just the kind of people I've been looking for," the

---

*Russian edict

czar replied. "Go tell them to come right away! They must per-
form a task for me; I will then make them my favorites and you
will be free to do what you like and sing as you please."

She bowed before the czar, went to fetch her sons, and sent
them to the monarch, who told them: "I have learned that you
possess gifts that are unique in the world. They will allow you to
get my daughter out of the sea and return her to me. I promise
that she will wed the eldest among you and that I will make you
all my favorites."

The brothers made their way to the seashore, and the one who
had the gift of hearing put his ear to the ground to discover where
the princess was being held. His attempt was crowned with success! He ordered his brother: "Suck up the sea at this spot!" which
he did. They could then see the czar's daughter sitting down and
weeping while the devil slept with his head on his knees. They
approached her, and the one who had the strength to carry ten
men picked her up and placed her on his shoulders. He stuffed
a frog in the devil's mouth so that he would wake up when it
croaked. He then picked his five brothers up and raced off like
a stag crossing through the mountains. The frog began croaking
and the devil awoke. He noticed that both the sea and the princess
had vanished, and exploded in rage.

Once he was fully awake he looked around and spotted the
six brothers fleeing with the czar's daughter. He set off in pursuit
and had soon almost caught up to them. "Regurgitate the sea!"
the five brothers said to the one who had swallowed it. He did
this and created a lake. But the devil flew over it and continued
in pursuit. "Brother, strike the ground with your fist to cause a
tower to spring forth, otherwise we are done for!" He complied
and they all shut themselves up inside. The devil went around and
around it not knowing what to do. He then said to them: "Very
well, you others. If you agree, let the princess show me her little
finger so that I can see one part of her one last time. Then you can

bring her wherever you wish." What to do? Should she show her finger or not? Finally they agreed, assuming that this would offer an easy solution to their predicament. They persuaded the princess to stick her finger through the keyhole. As soon as the devil saw it, he brought it to his mouth and sucked out the soul of the princess, who then died. He then took to his heels, but the brother who never missed his mark took aim and killed him. The one who knew how to resurrect the dead breathed into the czar's daughter, and she came back to life. They all accompanied her back to her father's palace, where he married her at once to the oldest brother. As promised, he made the other brothers his favorites.

AUGUST LESKIEN, *BALKANMÄRCHEN AUS BULGARIEN*
(IENA: EUGEN DIEDRICHES, 1915), 84–87.

ATU 513 C,* BP 3M 18–37, MLEX 297–301, EM 4, 1011–1021.

2. The Devil and the Fisherman's Daughters

Greece

Once upon a time there was an old fisherman who went to the seaside to catch some fish. When he tried to pull his net back out of the water, he pulled and pulled, but in vain. After much effort, he finally succeeded, and aside from a few small fish, he found an enormous iron key.[1] While he stared at it, a large, robust man appeared and told him: "The key you found belongs to me. I am Beelzebub, the master of the devils, and I live in hell where men live happily surrounded by treasure. Take the key and return to the shore Tuesday at the twelfth hour. You will find a door that you shall open. You shall enter and come to see me." With these words, he changed into a thick cloud of smoke and vanished beneath the earth. The old man returned home. During his meal, while he ate, with his children, the small fish he had caught, he showed them the large key, telling them of his adventure and adding that the following Tuesday he would bring them back some treasure.

Days passed and Tuesday came. At the appointed hour, the fisherman made his way to the shore with the key. He saw a large door that was a league in height and a third of a league wide. He opened it and entered a room where an old man was sitting. He was so old that his nose hung all the way down to his feet. His eyelashes and his white beard were so long that they covered him almost entirely. He held a scythe in his right hand, while in his left he held a rosary. He was counting its beads, of which there were thousands. Every minute a child popped out of him, and he devoured them immediately.* When he saw the fisherman, he spoke to him in a deep and solemn voice: "What have you come here to see? Many are those who have entered here without ever leaving again. Is it chance that has led you here, or is it your wish?"

"I have come to see your master," the fisherman replied, "the all-powerful."

"You risk regretting this, my son, for you will have to overcome many ordeals before reaching him. But since you have come in, the best thing you can do is to keep going. I'm going to give you some instructions. You must take this same path, and you will come to a large Lapsana bush.† It is guarded on one side by a proud and powerful lion and on the other by a very thin she-wolf almost dead from hunger. You will also hear voices that will terrify you and tell you that your family has died and other pieces of bad news. Don't hesitate and don't respond when you are called by name! Once you have gotten past the bush, you will make your way to a staircase that you will go down to find what you are looking for."

The fisherman followed the old man's instructions and found

---

*Would this be an avatar of Chronos?
†A flower from the sunflower family.

Beelzebub alone at home. He got up and asked the fisherman if he had any daughters. "I have three," the fisherman replied, "all of whom are motherless." The devil ordered one of his servants to give treasure to the old man, and once this was done, he told the fisherman to go back home and bring back one of his daughters the next day. The fisherman returned home overflowing with joy. When his children saw all the money that their father brought back, they all shouted together: "Father, buy me a headscarf, buy me a cardigan, buy me a woolly hat, buy me a dress!"

The next day, the eldest daughter lightheartedly set off with her father to the home of the lone devil. After the fisherman had once again been given all the money he could carry, he returned home, leaving his daughter to become the devil's wife. At lunchtime, Beelzebub went out, but only after he had given his wife a human foot by way of a meal. She could not bear to eat it and threw it into the midden. On his return, the devil asked her if she had eaten it and she nodded. He congratulated her, but because he did not believe her, he shouted: "Foot, where are you?"

"In the midden!"

Seeing that his wife had lied to him, he slapped her, which petrified her immediately. He then tossed her into a room in which all the other women he had treated the same way had been stored.

The next day, the fisherman returned. After giving him more money, the devil asked him to bring his second daughter. The old man obeyed, but the same thing befell his second daughter that had befallen her older sister. In the end, he brought his youngest daughter. After he left and mealtime was approaching, Beelzebub gave the young woman a human hand to serve as her lunch. She took it and tied it to her body. On his return, the devil asked her if she had eaten the hand. "Yes," she replied. The devil then called out, "Hand, where are you?" "In the body," it answered. From that moment the devil fully trusted the young woman, became infatuated with her, and married her. As he went away every day, he told his young bride that she could go into all the rooms of the house with the exception of one he showed her.[2]

One day while her husband was out, curiosity drove her to enter the forbidden room. What did she see? A large number of women, including her two sisters, all petrified. She was filled with despair, but she suddenly noticed that the word "Life" was written at the top of a wall, and under the inscription a bottle of brandy was hanging. She took it down, opened it, and sprinkled some on all the women in the room. They all came back to life.[3] She opened the door and they all fled from the devil's kingdom.

BERNHARD SCHMIDT, *GRIECHISCHE MÄRCHEN,*
SAGEN UND VOLKSLIEDER (LEIPZIG: TEUBNER, 1877), 122–25.

Schneller 32; Leskien 12; Widter 11, Gonzenbach 23; Wislocki 98; Obert 1; Asbjørnsen 42 (*De tre kongsdøtre i berget det blå*); Hahn 19, 73.

ATU 311, MLEX 317–21, EM 8, 1407–13.

3. The Devil's Boulders

Moravia

When someone travels from Kloboik* to Vsetin,† they will go through the village of Lideko, which is located in a pleasant valley.

One day, music was heard coming from the Lideko Inn. People were playing bagpipes and hand drums, and even though there was a regrettable lack of brandy, everybody was nonetheless feeling quite merry. When midnight was near, a stranger entered. After he took off the black coat that had enveloped him, he looked over the entire room. Dark black eyelashes topped two

---

*Klobouky u Burna, southern Moravia.
†Town located in the eastern Czech Republic.

sparkling eyes, and his black mustache gave him an imposing presence. His green jacket and feather had given the impression that he was a hunter. Amidst all the young women there was Kathy, a fatherless girl who had only her old mother. As she owned a pretty little house, fields, and meadows, was very pious, led a quiet life, and was quite cheerful, more than one of the local boys would have gladly wed her.

The stranger's gaze fell upon her and he went over to her side. While they danced they also chatted. She liked what he said and became smitten. He promised to visit her again soon, but, he added, as he was often busy with the hunt, he could only come at noon or midnight. He put on his coat, tossed a few twenty-cent coins to the musicians, and left shortly after midnight.

The stranger, whose name was Ladimil,[4] kept his word. But his late visits did not please the young maiden's mother, who always attended their get-togethers. She became suspicious of him as he always seemed unnaturally wary and alert, did not use holy water on arriving or leaving, and when, like her daughter, she blessed him as he left, he fled away like some wild creature.

Ladimil appeared one night around eleven o'clock and asked for Kathy's hand. For a half hour her mother refused on one pretext or another; finally, for he did not cease to beg her, she told him: "Fine, I will give you my daughter's hand but on one condition; if you do not fulfill it within the time set, the marriage will not happen." He rose out of his seat and said: "I am here, speak, I will do whatever you ask of me!" In the hope of preventing this marriage, the old woman said: "If, during the night, you can build a bridge over the valley from one mountain to the other, you shall marry my daughter;[5] if you cannot, never will you have her!"

"You're on!" replied the suitor with a demonic laugh as he rushed out of the house.

Once outside, he stamped his foot on the ground, the entire valley shook, and all at once an immense crowd of hooded people surrounded him in a circle. He ordered them to scatter over the entire region quickly and strangle all the roosters, and once that was done, to come help him by bringing the stones he needed to build a bridge. Heeding his command, they killed all the roosters. Hell's suitor, for this was the devil in person, had ordered them to do this so that no rooster could crow before the construction was finished—as everybody knows, roosters hold a great power over the devil and render harmless all the cruel tricks he has the habit of playing at midnight. Once the fowl had been reduced to silence, his companions from hell went to help their brother, but as there were no stones nearby, they first made their way into the forest from which they brought back gigantic boulders. With incredible speed the devil piled them up on the hills on both sides of the valley, and began to form the first arch.[6]

But there was a very old woman living in Lideko who owned a rooster. As she knew that the Black Tempter had a particular grudge against roosters since his vain attempt to tempt Saint Peter, she feared that her rooster might fall into the devil's claws and put both of them in his power. She had therefore hidden it beneath a watering trough in a secret place where no devil could find it. This was why it was the only rooster left alive after the infernal troop had gone off to slay all the roosters in the neighborhood.

As midnight approached, the devil had already built several arches and without a doubt would surely have finished his task within an hour and thereupon taken possession of the poor, innocent Kathy. But all at once the hidden rooster began to crow. See what happened! Immediately the monstrous boulders fell down, making a monstrous racket. The arches that had already been erected over the valley, the columns, and everything collapsed in a roar of thunder.

The stones on the heights of Lideko are the remnants of that construction. The devil who wanted to wed Kathy was petrified as a warning to all would-be seducers, and his horned head can still be seen today. Only those of his companions who could fly through the air survived; the others, who were pulling up stones in the forest, were also petrified and are still visible today.[7]

JOSEPH WENZIG, *WESTLAWISCHER MÄRCHENSCHATZ*
(LEIPZIG: LORCK, 1857), 174–79.

4. The Devil's Church

Romania

Once upon a time—and if this were not true, no one would ever talk about it and the story would have evaporated like a cloud in the wind—a king wished to build a church and hired eight masons and as many workers as were necessary. On the first day of construction the sovereign paid the site a visit to inspect the work. He returned the following week and saw that the work had not progressed. In a fury he demanded an explanation. The masons replied: "We are most unhappy because we have been busy and don't know who comes every night to destroy the work we did during the day."

The devil, dressed as a mason, then came along and told the king he could construct the building in just one night. These words were music to the ears of the king who asked: "What is your price?"

"Whoever enters the church first will belong to me."

The king had a splendid daughter whose beauty even eclipsed that of the sun. In the morning, the church had been finished. All that was missing was the cross. People should have perceived its absence, but the building was so beautiful that no one noticed. However, the princess did notice and raced into the church to see if it had been set up above the altar. When she entered, the devil grabbed her as had been agreed with her father, and he placed her in a coffin next to the altar. In terror, the king suddenly realized who had built the church, and in his distress begged the devil to post guards permanently next to the casket from dawn to dusk. Nothing happened to those who kept watch during the day, but those who kept guard at night vanished, devoured by the demon.

The day finally came when the king had only one company of soldiers left. There were two lads in this company, one a sergeant and the other a corporal, whose twelve-year service had come to an end this sad year. They went to ask the king for a few kreutzers to cover their travel expenses. When they got to the door, the sergeant told his companion: "You go in first, corporal, I don't dare."

"Sergeant, you go in first, you are bigger than me," the corporal replied, and the sergeant went in.

"Good day, sire."

"What do you want?"

"I have served twelve years; I am now free of my obligations and I don't have a single kreutzer for going back home."

"Were you a good soldier?"

"Yes."

"Did you obey your orders?"

"Yes."

"Then give me a slap." Panicked, the sergeant replied: "How can I slap Your Majesty?" The monarch then slapped him and chased him out. The corporal asked him: "Did you get anything?"

"Yes, now it's your turn, so he can give you some, too."

On entering, the corporal greeted the king, who responded: "What do you want?"

"I have served twelve years; I am now free of my obligations and I don't have the smallest kreutzer for going back home."

"Were you a good soldier?"

"Yes."

"Did you obey your orders?"

"Yes."

"Then give me a slap."

The corporal did as he was asked and made the monarch see stars.

"Well done!" the king shouted, and gave him one hundred florins.

The corporal thanked the sovereign, and accompanied the sergeant to an inn to have a drink. The corporal paid for his drink and asked the sergeant to do the same so they could leave. The latter explained to him that all he had gotten was a slap. "But how is this possible? He gave me one hundred florins." The sergeant then told him what had happened to him. It was then that a patrol entered to fetch the corporal.

When he was before the king, the corporal asked him: "Sire, what is your command?"

"I have seen that you were a good soldier and you know what happened to my daughter. If a lad can be found who is capable of spending three nights in a row in the church, he will free my daughter, and I will give him her hand in marriage and half of my kingdom. As I've seen your true worth, it occurred to me that you might be the man for the situation."

"Sire, I am going to try."

That evening, as ten o'clock sounded, the corporal made his way alone to the church, and prayed to God with a pure heart. At eleven o'clock his guardian angel appeared and asked: "Are you there?"

"Yes!"

"Fear nothing. When midnight sounds, the princess possessed by the devil[*] will come out of her coffin, and you will have to hide behind the altar."

At the time cited, the princess emerged from her coffin and started looking for soldiers all over the church, including the steeple, but did not even cast a single glance behind the altar. When

---

*The text uses the word *năzdrăvan,* "wicked."

one o'clock sounded, having exhausted all her strength, she lay back down while crying: "Little father, little father, dog that you are, you sent me nothing to eat!" In the morning the corporal left the church while smoking a cigar.

That night at ten o'clock he returned to the church and sent the other guards away. At eleven o'clock his angel showed up: "Are you there?"

"Yes!"

"Hide in the steeple tonight, for she will look behind the altar."

At midnight, the princess got up and looked without finding anything. After an hour had passed she returned to her coffin. "Little father, little father, dog that you are, you sent me nothing to eat!" The lad emerged from his hiding place, lit a cigar, and strolled around the church until morning.

The third night his angel asked him: "Are you there?"

"Yes!"

"Don't hide tonight and stand near the coffin."

At midnight, the coffin creaked and the corporal planted himself in front of it. The coffin creaked a second time and the soldier lay down on the ground. The princess looked everywhere and found nothing. The lad then stretched out in the coffin. When one o'clock sounded the princess returned to lie down, but found the soldier there and asked him: "Who are you?"

"Me!"

"Who is me?"

"Me."

"Get out of the coffin!"

"I will get out after you have repeated to me the first thing your father taught you."

It was only at his third request that she answered: "The Our Father," and was freed. They embraced and she told him: "You will be my husband and I will be your wife."

That morning they left the church together. The guards announced to the sovereign that the lad who had slapped him had freed his daughter. Four stallions were hitched to a carriage and the king went to the church. "Did you save my daughter?" he asked.

"Yes, sire."

"Her hand and half my kingdom are yours, then," the king said, and they entered the church for the betrothal.

After the ceremony, the young man's guardian angel returned and took the princess aside. He pulled out one of her hairs, divided it in half and pulled out twelve devils that he cast away, thereby exorcising the maiden. He then led her back to her fiancé and said: "Take her, she is now as pure as you." A luxurious wedding was celebrated. A brioche was placed on the tail of every dog in attendance,* and if they yet live, they are still together today.

PAULINE SCHULLERUS, *RUMÄNISCHE VOLKSMÄRCHEN AIS DEM MITTLEREN HARSBACHTAL* (BUCHAREST: KRITERION, 1977), 321–26.

📖 Widter 13

ATU 307, BP 3, 531–37, MLEX 560–63, EM 10, 1355–63.

5. The Devil Marries Three Sisters

Veneto, Italy

One day, the devil felt an urge to get married. He left hell, took on the shape of a handsome young man,[8] and built himself a large, beautiful dwelling. When it was finished and handsomely

---

*This phrase can only be understood in reference to a fossilized Romanian expression reflecting this curious custom: "there where the dogs have brioches on their tails" (*acolo unde umblă câinii cu covrigi în coadă*). It refers to a nonexistent place, with abundant wealth, where the lazy can get whatever they want without doing a thing. We would like to thank Emanuela Timotin, who shared this with us.

furnished, he started visiting a family that had three pretty daughters, and wooed the oldest. She liked him, her parents were delighted to see their daughter make such a good match, and a short time later the wedding was celebrated. Once he had his new wife in his home, he gave her a small, tastefully arranged bouquet, and showed her all the rooms in the house before ending this tour in front of a closed door. "The whole house is at your disposal," he told her, "I just ask that you never ever open this door."[9]

Of course the young woman promised she wouldn't, and then waited impatiently for him to go out. The next day, when the devil had left the house on the pretext of going hunting, she went to the forbidden door as fast as she could, opened it, and found a flaming abyss behind it. Its flames sprang toward her, wilting the bouquet on her chest. When her husband returned, he asked her if she had kept her promise. Without a moment's hesitation she replied, "Yes," but when he saw the flowers he realized that she was lying and said, "I'm going to satisfy your curiosity with no delay. Come, I'm going to show you what's behind this door." When he opened it, he gave her a shove and sent her plummeting into hell,[10] then shut the door again.

Several months later he asked for the second daughter's hand in marriage and got it. But everything turned out exactly the same as it had with the first wife.

Finally he asked for the hand of the youngest sister, but this woman, who was quite intelligent, thought: "He surely killed my two sisters, but this will be a brilliant match for me. I am going to try to be luckier than them." She accepted his offer of marriage. After the wedding, her husband gave her a pretty little bouquet and forbid her from opening the famous door.

No less curious than her sisters, she opened the forbidden door once the devil had gone hunting, but took the precaution of sticking her little bouquet in water. Behind the door she saw hell and her two sisters. "Alas," she said to herself, "I thought I was marrying an ordinary man, and he's the devil! How can I get rid of him?" She carefully pulled her sisters out of hell and hid them. On his return, the devil immediately cast a glance at the bouquet that she had put on again. When he saw it was so fresh, he didn't ask any questions and, reassured about his secret, he only loved her all the more.

Several days later, she asked him to carry three chests to her parents' house without setting them down on the way and stopping to rest. "You must keep your word," she added, "for I will check to make sure that you do." The devil promised to do everything and anything she asked. The next day, she put one of her sisters in a chest, and loaded it upon her husband's shoulders. The devil, who was of course very strong, but also very lazy and scarcely accustomed to work, soon had his fill of carrying the heavy chest, and wanted to take a rest before he even left their street. But she shouted at him: "Don't put it down, I can see you!" He turned the corner of the street, smoldering with resentment from carrying the chest, and thought to himself: "She cannot see me anymore. I'm going to take a little break." But he had barely come to a halt when the sister yelled from inside the chest: "Don't put it down. I can see you." Swearing a blue streak, he carried the chest into the next street and started to place it under a porch, but the voice spoke out again: "Don't put it down, you rogue, I can see you!"

"What good eyes my wife must have," he told himself. "She sees even after I went round a corner as if I had just gone straight, and through all the arches as if they were made of glass." This is how he arrived at his mother-in-law's house all sweaty and exhausted. He set down the chest as fast as he could, then raced back home to have a large breakfast.

The same thing happened the next day with the second chest. On the third day, it was the youngest daughter's turn to be carried back to her parents' place. She crafted a mannequin that she clad in her clothes and set it up on the balcony as if she wanted to watch her husband from afar. She then slipped into the chest and had her servant place it on the devil's shoulders. "Plague," he said to himself, "this chest is even heavier than the others, and as my wife is sitting on the balcony, I will have even less chance of stopping to rest!" At the cost of some strong exertions, he carried it to his mother-in-law's, then, muttering, and with an aching back, he raced back home to get a solid breakfast.

But contrary to the other times, he did not find either his wife or breakfast waiting for him. "Marguerite, where can you be?" he called. But there was no answer. After searching through all the hallways, he looked out the window and spotted the mannequin on a balcony.* "Marguerite, are you sleeping? I'm dying of exhaustion, and I'm as hungry as a wolf!" Again there was no response at all. "If you don't come down right now, I will come up there to fetch you," he screamed in rage. The mannequin didn't budge. Full of wrath, he made his way onto the balcony and gave it a slap that sent its head flying. He then realized that the head was only a stick topped by a wool hat, and the body was made from rags. Beside himself, he went back down, and found only his wife's open jewelry box. "Ah," he shouted, "someone abducted her and stole her jewels!" He immediately raced over to his in-laws' house to tell them his tale of woe. But when he got there he saw, to his great stupefaction, his wives, the three sisters, sitting on the balcony above the door. They all thumbed their noses at him and made fun of him. Three wives at once! The devil got so scared that he took off as fast as he could. Since then, he has had no desire to get married.

GEORG WIDTER, ADAM WOLF, "VOLKSMÄRCHEN AUS VENETIEN," *JAHRBUCH FÜR ROMANISCHE UND ENGLISCHE LITERATUR* 8 (LEIPZIG, 1866): 148–154.

---

*In the text, Widter writes these expressions in dialect: *poggiolo* (balcony); *stracco da can* (dead of exhaustion); *una fame da lov* (hungry as a wolf).

📖 Schneller 88–90; Gonzenbach 23; Wlislocki 98; Obert 1; Asbjørnsen 42 (*De tre kongsdøtre i berget det blå*); Hahn 19, 73.

ATU 311, BP 1, 398–412; EM 8, 1407–13; MLEX 317–21. HANS JÖRG UTHER, "DER FRAUENMÖRDER BLAUBART UND SEINE ARTVERWANDTEN," *SCHWEIZERISCHES ARCHIV FÜR VOLKSKUNDE* 84 (1988): 34–54. REIDAR T. CHRISTENSEN, "THE SISTERS AND THE TROLL," *STUDIES IN FOLKLORE* (1957): 24–39.

The comparison of various European traditions shows that the devil is interchangeable with a wizard (Germany), a miner (Denmark), a man who changes into a horse at night (Scotland), and a dog-headed man (Greece). The forbidden room is full of blood and women's corpses in the German and Scottish tales, which brings Bluebeard to mind. The flower bouquet, meanwhile, is an egg (Germany) or an apple (Denmark) from which the blood won't disappear.

In a Danish story, a troll replaces the devil. Three sisters are put to the test by a malevolent being: the first two fail but the more intelligent third sister is able to resuscitate her sisters.[11]

CHAPTER II

THE DEVIL AND HIS FAMILY

1. The Devil's Wife

Italian Tyrol

A royal couple had an only child, a beautiful daughter who greatly valued beautiful clothing and adornments. One day she found a louse, and as she did not know what it was, she ran to ask her mother. Her mother answered her question and told her: "Shut the louse inside a box and feed it. Once it has grown big enough, we will make a pair of gloves with its skin, and whichever one of your suitors can guess what animal skin this is will become your husband."

The princess followed her mother's advice. The repulsive beast was so well-fed that she had to replace its box several times with a larger one. Once it had grown big enough, gloves were made from its skin, and they were displayed for all to see. It was explicitly stated that the person who could guess the origin of this skin would marry the princess. Numerous princes and knights tried to solve this mystery, but none managed to do so. Finally, a stranger appeared who gave the correct answer, and he married the princess. He then took her back to his home. It was the devil in person.

A short time later he had to leave on a journey. Before he left he gave his wife all the keys to the house and permission to open the rooms, with the exception of only one. In his absence, she could not resist her curiosity, and opened the forbidden door. She saw hell and in its flames she saw her grandfather and her grandmother groaning and reaching their hands out to her. She barely avoided falling in herself, but had the strength to jump back and shut the door. She fell ill from fright and had to stay in bed, realizing that she had married the devil. After she got better, she was sitting alone in her room when a pigeon from her father's house knocked on her window with its beak. She quickly wrote a note on a piece of paper: "Father, save me, I am the devil's wife," and tied it to the pigeon's neck. It flew away and returned after several days with a note from her father warning her to be on her guard night and day, and telling her that he would come to rescue her.

Accompanied by valiant warriors, the king set off to go to the devil's house and free his daughter, fully aware that this would be difficult and fearful that he would not succeed. On the way there, he met a man who was staring far off into the distance. "What are you looking at?" the monarch asked him.

"I have such sharp eyesight," the other replied, "that I can even see inside the devil's house."

"What is the devil's wife doing?" the sovereign asked urgently.

"She is sitting in her room, weeping."

"Come with me," said the king, "and I will reward you well."

While continuing their journey, they ran into a man who was listening intently without moving a muscle. "What are you listening to?" the king asked.

"I have such keen hearing[1] that I can even hear what is happening in the devil's house."

"What is the devil's wife doing?"

"I can hear her sighing."

"Accompany me," said the king, "you will be well paid."

They set off again and met a third man who was so strong that he could raise the largest and heaviest front gates without making a sound, and the king hired him. They then came across a fourth person whose eyesight, hearing, and strength were normal but who could walk so softly that even the man with keen hearing could barely hear him. They then all set off again together[2] and Sharp Sight (the first man) showed them the shortest way there. When they reached the devil's house, night had already fallen. The second companion, Keen Ears, perked up his ears and said: "The devil, who has returned in the meantime, has gone to bed and is snoring, but his wife is awake and sighing." The strong man pulled the gate off its hinges, making little sound. "Shh, shh," said Keen Ears, hearing that the devil was a little restless in his sleep, and had turned over to the other side. "Good," he said a few moments later, "he has begun to snore again and is deep in sleep." Light Foot (the fourth man) went to fetch the princess, and they then all took flight, getting assurance now and then from Keen Ears through the night that the devil was still sleeping and snoring. By morning they had gotten back to the palace.

Delighted, the king kept his word and made the four rescuers rich and happy men for the rest of their lives.

LA SPOSA DEL DIAVOLO, CHRISTIAN SCHNELLER,
MÄRCHEN UND SAGEN AUS WÄLSCHTIROL.
EIN BEITRAG ZUR DEUTSCHEN SAGENKUNDE
(INNSBRUCK: WAGNER'SCHE
UNIVERSITÄTS-BUCH-HANDLUNG, 1867), 86–88.

BP 2, 79–96, MLEX 317–321; 1081–84. EM 8, 1407–13.

2. The Devil's Mother-in-Law

Spain

A long time ago in a place named Villagañanes there lived an old widow who was as ugly as the hideous sergeant of Utrera,* as thin and dry as a clump of needlegrass,† as old as walking, and as yellow as the fever of the same name. Furthermore, her character was so unbearable it would even have tried the patience of Job. She was called Dame Holopherne and as soon as she set foot in the street, all the urchins took flight. However, she was as clean as pure spring water and as industrious as an ant. This is why the laziness and indolence of her daughter Panfila filled her with dismay. This girl was as apathetic as her godfather; even an earthquake could not have made her budge. She was the reason why Dame Holopherne cursed and grumbled every day, from the moment when God spread light at dawn to the evening when He took it back. "Your character is as feeble as Holland tobacco is mild," she told her daughter, "and it would take a pair of oxen to get you out of bed. You flee from work as if it were the plague, and your only pleasure is to sit by the window like a monkey. Like the god Cupid, love is your only concern, but I'm going to teach you how to behave and rule you with an iron hand, and do so quicker than the wind!" When Panfila heard this sermon, she got up, yawning. After stretching she made her way to the door that opened onto the street,‡ without her mother noticing.

---

*We don't know the origin of this comparison, used by several authors, including Pedro Antonio de Alarcón, *El Sombrero de tres picos* (Madrid: Perez Dubrull, 1882), chap. XIV. The following study—Shirley Lease Arora, *Proverbial Comparisons and Related Expressions in Spanish* (Berkeley, Los Angeles: University of California Press, 1977, Folklore Studies, 29, 419 *ff.*)—didn't succeed in clarifying this.

†This is a hardy herbaceous plant that grows in arid regions.

‡*Se iba á la puerta de la calle.*

As this was happening, Dame Holoherne was diligently sweeping the room, accompanying each sweep of her broom with a soliloquy: "In my time, girls worked like mules"—fritch, froutch said the broom—"and they lived cloistered like nuns"—fritch, froutch—"but today they are mad as hatters"—fritch, froutch—"lazing about"—fritch, froutch—"thinking only of their suitors"—fritch, froutch—"all good for nothings!" While she was soliloquizing she spotted her daughter by the door, and in the blink of an eye began vigorously smacking her daughter's back with the broom. Her daughter—what a marvel—began to run. Dame Holoherne stuck her nose out the door and as usual sent everyone fleeing, particularly Panfila's suitor, who seemed to have wings on his feet. "Cursed young little miss in heat!" Dame Holopherne yelled. "I'm going to break all your bones!* What are you looking for with your inappropriate behavior?"

"Marriage, Mother."

"What are you saying? Get married? You're stark raving mad!† Never while I'm alive!"

"But weren't you married, just like your mother and your grandmother?"

"I have much regretted it. If I'd stayed single, I would not have brought you into the world, perverted girl! And even if your mother, your grandmother, and your great-grandmother were married, I don't want you to do the same thing, anymore than I would want my granddaughters and great-granddaughters to do it. Understand?" Mother and daughter spent their days engaged in these bittersweet exchanges, with the sole result that the mother became a little crabbier everyday, and the daughter a little more insolent.

---

*Te he de romper cuantos huesos tienes en tu cuerpe. A detail absent from the German translation by Wilhelm Hosäus, Spanische Volkslieder und Volksreime; Spanische Volks- und Kindermärchen; Einfache Blüthen religiöser Poesie (Paderborn: Ferdinand Schöningh, 1862), 157–74.
†Loca de atar, left out by W. Hosäus.

One day, when Dame Holopherne was doing the laundry and the water had started to boil, she asked her daughter to help her pour the cauldron of hot water on the laundry. Her daughter's head was somewhere else because she was listening to her lover singing in the street:

> *I would like your love*
> *and your mother opposes it;*
> *That old demon*
> *Meddles in everything.**

This fine speech offered Panfila something more pleasant than the cauldron of boiling water, and leaving her mother to shout herself hoarse, she went to the door. Seeing that her daughter wasn't coming and the wait was dragging on, Dame Holopherne decided to pour the water on the laundry by herself. But because she was so thin and not very strong, she dropped the cauldron and burned one of her feet. "Cursed girl, doubly cursed be she!" she yelled. "She's as mean as a basilisk and thinks of nothing but her lover. May God give her the devil for a husband!"

A short time later, a suitor, the likes of whom are rare, introduced himself to Panfila. He was young, light-skinned, blonde, well-raised, and had a bulging purse. There was never anything to criticize him for, and even Dame Holopherne could not come up with an argument against him. Panfila was crazed with joy. Preparations were made for the wedding, accompanied by the inevitable grumblings of the fiancé's future mother-in-law. Everything was going off without a hitch but the *vox populi,* as infallible as conscience, castigated the stranger, despite his appearance as a friendly, generous sycophant. He spoke well and sang even better, and would shake the brown,

---

*Verses absent from the French and German translations (*Contes andalous*) that appeared in *Les Grands Auteurs de toutes les littératures,* 2e series, vol. 3, 1888.

calloused hands of the peasants with his own slender, ring-adorned hands. The peasants felt absolutely disrespected, and were not at all seduced by his affability. Their minds were a bit crude, of course, but they had solid good sense, as solid as their hands. "I have to confess," said old father Blas, "that this individual who calls me Señor, as if I was an arrogant buffoon who wanted to be called Señor, seems shady to me. What do you say?"

"He came to me," said old father Gilles, "and stretched out his paw as if we were old pals, and he called me 'citizen'—me who has never left my village."

In similar fashion, Dame Holopherne watched her future son-in-law with growing suspicion. She had the impression that some ill-omened protuberances were hiding beneath his innocent blond curls. She anxiously recalled the curse she had cast on her daughter on that less-than-fondly remembered day, when she learned how much harm could be caused by being burned with boiling water.

The wedding day, for which Dame Holopherne had made cakes as well as thoughts, some sweet and others bitter, arrived. There was a large olla podrida* for lunch, and a malevolent plan for dinner. And as an accompaniment for everything, Dame Holopherne had prepared a generous cask of wine and a not-so-generous procedure to follow.

When the newlyweds decided to go to their room, Dame Holopherne called her daughter and told her: "Once you have gone in, close all the doors and windows and cork up every crack. Then take a consecrated olive branch and hit your husband with it until I tell you to stop. This is a customary ceremony in every marriage, which means that once in the bedroom, it's the woman who's in charge. Furthermore, this ceremony helps her establish and cement her rule."

Silly Panfila believed her mother and obeyed her for once in

---

*A meat and vegetable stew that is simmered a long time.

her life. She followed the advice of the cunning old woman to the letter. As soon as the young groom caught sight of the olive branch in his wife's hand, he tried to flee. But how? Doors and windows were bolted, and all the cracks blocked off. His only option was the keyhole. He dove into it as if it were a carriage gate. My listeners will have realized, just as Dame Holopherne had, that the fashionable young groom with his blond hair and pale skin was none other than the devil. He believed that Dame Holopherne's curse gave him justification to enjoy the celebrations and delicacies of a wedding before carrying his wife off to hell, thereby doing for himself what so many husbands had begged him to do for them.

Although it is public knowledge that this gentleman is exceptionally wily, with this mother-in-law he finally met someone more cunning than he—and Dame Holopherne is not the only person like that! Hardly had His Lordship slid through the keyhole and congratulated himself for having found a way to escape when he found himself prisoner in a large bottle that his foresighted mother-in-law had stuck in front of the keyhole. The old woman hermetically sealed the bottle, and for the moment there was no possibility of escape.

With the sweetest words, the most humble entreaties, and moving gestures, her son-in-law begged her to restore his freedom. He pointed out to her that she was acting arbitrarily and not respecting the rights of the people. Through her despotic actions she was violating the constitution. Dame Holopherne did not fall for this ruse. Speeches and big words made no impression on her. She took the bottle with its contents up to the top of a mountain, which she scaled energetically, before placing it at the peak where it sat like a rooster's comb. The lady then parted, shaking her fist at her son-in-law.

His Lordship spent ten years there, and what a ten years these were, gentlemen! All at once the world was as calm as a sea of oil, everyone minded their own business and did not meddle in things that did not concern them. No one coveted the position, the wife, or the goods of his neighbor. Stealing was a meaningless word, weapons rusted and gunpowder was used for fireworks, and the mad no longer raved but simply kept themselves amused. These ten years were a veritable golden age, with only one regrettable incident occurring: lawyers died of starvation.

Alas, this state of things could not last; everything comes to an end in this world, except for the elegant speeches of politicians. Here is how this happy decade met its end: A soldier named Briones was given leave so he could go to his village. His route took him by the mountain where Dame Holopherne's son-in-law was living. He spent his time cursing all mothers-in-law, past, present, and future, that malicious tribe that he swore he would exterminate by abolishing marriage—and by writing pamphlets on the invention of detergent.

When Briones reached the foot of the mountain, he did not want to make a detour and told the mule drivers* accompanying him: "If it won't move out of my path, I will climb it no matter how tall it is, even if I give myself a bump by colliding with the sky." He eventually reached the summit, and was quite surprised to find the bottle. He picked it up and turned it to the light, and when he saw the devil inside, whom fasting, seclusion, sorrow, and heat had shrunk to the size of a plum, cried out: "What little beast, what kind of monster, what wonder could this be?"

"I'm an honorable and deserving devil," the other replied affably and humbly. "The perversity of a wicked, felonious mother-in-law (if I could only get my claws on her!) has held me captive here. Free me, valiant warrior, and I will grant you whatever you wish."

"I wish to be relieved of my military obligations," Briones replied without hesitating.

---

*Left out by W. Hosäus.

"And so you shall, but free me quickly, for it's a monstrous mistake in this revolutionary period to hold the revolutionary-in-chief prisoner."

Briones pulled out the cork, and a mephitic vapor immediately rose up into his brain. He sneezed and quickly recorked the bottle so forcefully that he trapped the devil howling in pain. "What are you doing, you miserable worm, a thousand times more duplicitous than my mother-in-law?"

"I want to add another condition to our agreement. It seems to me that the favor I am going to do for you truly deserves it."

"What is it, you scoundrel of a liberator?"

"I demand four *douros** every day for as long as I live. Think on it seriously; your only choice is to get out or remain imprisoned."

"By Satan, Lucifer, and Beelzebub!" screamed the devil in rage. "Greedy wretch, I don't have any money!"

"How about that, what a fine excuse for a gentleman as powerful as you. This answer would be suitable for a minister, but is unworthy of you and hurts my ears."

"Since you don't believe me, let me out so I can help you find money, just as I've already helped many other people. That's all I can do for you. Let me out, let me out!"

"Steady, steady," Briones replied, "there is nothing pressing us and no one misses you. I'm going to hold you firmly by the tail and will not let you go until you have kept your promise."

"You don't trust me? How insolent!" the devil shouted.

"No!" Briones responded.

"What you are asking is an offense against my dignity," the prisoner replied, with all the haughtiness a dried-up prune can show.

"Very well, I'm leaving," the soldier said.

Seeing him moving away, the devil squirmed furiously in the bottle and yelled: "Come back, come back, dear friend!" while

---

*A douro is a 5 *pesata* coin.

grumbling to himself: "May a four-year-old bull gore you with its horns, old rogue!" He then went on out loud: "Come here, come here, charitable creature, come near and free me! Hold me by my tail or by my nose, it doesn't matter, brave soldier," and he added *in petto**: "I will not forget to get my revenge, vile soldier, and if I can't manage to marry you off to Dame Holopherne's daughter, I will at least arrange matters so that you burn next to her on the same pyre!"

Briones turned back, opened the bottle, and Dame Holopherne's son-in-law emerged from it like a chick from an egg, first his head, then his limbs, and finally his tail, which the soldier firmly grabbed despite the devil's attempt to retract it. The former captive, all paralyzed and contorted, shook himself, limbered up, extended his arms and legs, and they set off for the king's palace. The devil trudged ahead while Briones walked right behind him, holding onto his tail.

Once in the city, the devil said to Briones, "I'm going to slip inside the body of the princess whose father adores her, and cause her such pains that no doctor will be able to relieve them. Show up at the palace and offer to make her better, on condition that they pay you four douros a day for the rest of your life. I will leave her body, she will be cured, and I will no longer owe you anything." The devil believed he'd thought this out carefully and anticipated everything, but what he failed to foresee was that Briones would not let go of his tail when he tried to leave. "Most gentle gentleman," said Briones, "four douros is a trifle unworthy of either of us with respect to the favor I am doing for you. Find a way to be more generous! Let me just add in passing that this would do you great honor, for, pardon my frankness, the world doesn't have a particularly good opinion of you."

"If only I could carry you," the devil muttered to himself, "but I'm so weak and dazed that I can hardly stand. I must be patient, something men believe to be a virtue. I now understand why so many people have fallen into my power: they don't have

---

*In private

any patience. Let's get on with it then, damn you! You will step from the gallows right into my infernal cauldron. We are going to return to Naples to find the fitting means to satisfy your greed."

The princess was writhing on her couch in pain. The sovereign was dismayed and anxious. Briones introduced himself with all the arrogance of someone who knows the devil is helping him. The king accepted his offer, but only on condition that if he did not heal the princess after the three days he promised so confidently, he would be hanged. Sure he would succeed, the soldier raised no objection. Unfortunately, the devil had heard all this and was hopping up and down with joy that such a wonderful opportunity to avenge himself had been offered him. His exuberant movements in the princess's body caused her to scream in pain and for someone to send the doctor away. The same thing happened the next day. Briones realized that the devil was playing his own game, but he was not a man who lost his head easily. When the so-called doctor arrived the third day, the gallows had already been erected in front of the palace gates. He entered the chamber of the princess, whose pains intensified immediately. As on the previous days, she asked that the charlatan be driven away. "I haven't tried everything yet," Briones said gravely. "May it please Your Grace to wait a moment." He left and commanded in the princess's name that all the bells in the city be rung continuously. When he went back into her bedroom, the devil, who felt as if he were in mortal agony, but was at the same time curious to learn whom they were ringing for, asked which saint was being celebrated. "They are sounding in honor of your mother-in-law, whom I've invited to come here!" Immediately the Evil One took flight,[3] so quickly that not even a sunbeam could have caught him. Proud as a rooster and extremely happy, Briones let out a hearty cock-a-doodle-do.

First publication, Fernan Caballero
(pen name of Cecilia Francisca Josefa Böhl de Faber,
1796–1877), *Cuentos y poesías populares andaluzas*.

(SEVILLE: LA REVISTA MERCANTIL, 1859), 148–163.
TRANSLATION/ANONYMOUS ADAPTATION:*
CONTES ANDALOUS, APPEARING IN LES GRANDS AUTEURS DE
TOUTES LES LITTÉRATURES, 2ND SERIES, VOL. 3, 1888.
WE TRANSLATED THE TEXT PUBLISHED IN CUENTOS,
ADIVINANZAS Y REFRANES POPULARES, RECOPILACIÓN
(MADRID: SÁENZ DE JUBERA, HERMANOS, 1921), 149–163.[4]

ATU 1164 A.

3. The Devil for a Brother-in-Law

Switzerland

One day a traveling apprentice came to an inn. As he had walked quite a bit over the previous days, he was tired and wanted to get a good rest, but was not thinking that his wallet did not hold enough to pay for it. When one evening the innkeeper realized his guest was penniless, he told him: "My friend, you are no longer tired, so be kind enough to skedaddle tomorrow; here's your little bill." The lad trembled and begged his host to wait at least until the next day to be paid. "It will only be one more day," he added.

"Fine, but be careful of the Inn of the Black Tower. That's where those who eat and drink more than the contents of their money bag will afford are carted away to."

Once the innkeeper stepped out, the apprentice threw himself on his bed, but could not get a wink of sleep all night because his worries kept gnawing away at him. Suddenly a dark silhouette approached his bed, making it clear from the start that he was the devil. "Fear nothing, dear companion, a favor deserves another

---

*Considered an adaptation, because it often departs from the text.

favor in return. If you agree to help me with a trifling little matter, I will get you out of your predicament."

"What would I have to do?"

"You only have to stay in this inn for seven years," said the devil, "and I will give you piles and piles of money, all you need to cover the expenses of a pleasing lifestyle. In return, all I ask is that you don't wash yourself or comb your hair. Nor are you to cut your hair and nails."

"This bargain sounds as good as any I could possibly get," thought the apprentice, and shook hands with his benefactor.

The next day, the innkeeper received cash on the barrelhead, and also received advance payment for all future expenses. Year after year, the boy stayed at the inn and spent his money without counting it. He became as filthy as a pig, and his appearance was repulsive.

One fine morning, a merchant who had three pretty daughters came to the innkeeper's place. The merchant was a neighbor. He had made a lot of deals that had not panned out, and no longer knew what saint to turn to. He came to visit the innkeeper to share his distress. "Listen," the innkeeper told him, "there may be a way to help you. A stranger has been living in one of my rooms for more than six years. He's an odd duck who never cuts his hair or beard and is as ugly as the seven capital sins, but has money to spare and never refuses anything, so go see him. I've long noticed that he's often leering in the direction of your place. Who knows? He might be harboring designs on one of your daughters." This advice seemed quite reasonable to the merchant. He went up to the apprentice's room, and they soon came to an agreement: the young man would extricate him from his financial mess in return for the hand of one of his daughters. But when they went to find the three daughters to inform them of the bargain, the eldest took off laughing: "Fie, father! What horror are you bringing to see us here? I'd rather drown than marry him!" The second reacted no kindlier and screamed: "Ugh, Father! What kind of monster are you bringing to us! I'd rather hang than marry him!" In contrast, the youngest daughter said, "He is ready to save you, Father, so he must be a gallant man. I accept." She kept her eyes lowered without looking at him, but he already liked her intensely, and they set a date for the wedding.

The seven years that the devil had set for the young man came to an end, and on the day of the wedding, a splendid carriage, sparkling with gold and precious stones, appeared in front of the merchant's house. The apprentice, who was now a young, rich, and elegant nobleman, stepped out. His fiancée felt as if a huge weight had been take off of her, and cries of joy arose. It was a long procession that made its way to the church for the wedding because the merchant and the innkeeper had invited all their relatives. Only the two sisters of the happy fiancée were absent: one had drowned herself in a fit of rage, and the other had hanged herself. While coming out of the church, the groom saw, for the first time in seven years, the devil perched on a roof, laughing in satisfaction:

> *Brother-in-law, this is how it worked out*
> *You got one and I got two!*

OTTO SUTERMEISTER,
KINDER-UND HAUSMÄRCHEN AUS DER SCHWEIZ
(AARAU: H. R. SAUERLÄNDER, 1869), 80–83.

4. How the Devil Played the Flute

Germany

One day, when the devil was getting bored in hell, he decided to take a leisure trip to Earth. So he would not be alone, something for which he had little taste because he quite liked to have company, he brought his youngest son, a little dark-colored rascal who was intensely curious. They left through a cave and came out in a forest, which made the little imp as happy as could be. He hopped and jumped from here to there, climbed trees and hung upside down by his tail like a monkey, and generally horsed around. They came to a large oak tree where a man dressed in green was sleeping. A hunting bag was hanging from the branches, and out of it were sticking all sorts of animals: hares, woodcocks, and wild ducks. A rifle was placed next to the game bag. The little devil raced over and, examining it closely, picked it up. He asked his father what it was. Furrowing his brow, he replied: "My son, it's a flute. When men play it, the game comes running to them, and all they have to do is catch them."

"I want to see that!" shouted the imp. "Play me a tune."

"It takes two, son, one to blow and the other to move his fingers."

"You blow and I'll poke," said the imp, and his father was forced, whether he liked it or not, to bring the rifle barrel to his mouth as he had explained the whole affair to his son. The old devil blew and the imp kept poking, poking, poking, but no sound came out. "Idiot, you have to press on the keys!" his father shouted. His son pressed the trigger, a shot went off, and his father collapsed because the bullet had gone down his throat. The imp fled in terror. His father soon recovered and ran right behind his son, as the detonation had woken the man up. "That wasn't a pretty sound," said the little devil. "You didn't press the right key! And because the flute was dusty, all the dust went down my throat."

Johann Wilhelm Wolf, *Deutsche Hausmärchen*
(Göttingen: Dieterische Buchhandlung,
Leipzig: Vogel, 1851), n° 53.

5. My Godfather the Devil

Switzerland

A poor day laborer had the devil as his godfather, but he didn't know it. One day the Evil One came in search of him and said: "How poor you are! Very well, I'm going to give you a large field that you will cultivate for both of us, on the condition that what grows under the ground belongs to me and what grows over the ground belongs to you." The day laborer accepted this bargain, worked the field, and sowed it with wheat. It grew mightily, and when the time came he harvested it. He invited his godfather to take what had grown underground. The devil found nothing but roots, and realized that he had been duped by his godson. He then said: "Our agreement is null and void. If you want to continue farming, we need to reverse the terms: what grows above ground will be mine, and what grows below will belong to you." The peasant agreed and planted the entire field with potatoes. The harvest was magnificent and he alerted his godfather to come harvest what had grown above ground, namely the leaves, while he gathered enough potatoes to fill many bushels, which brought him a lot of money. The devil realized he was always going to lose at this game, and swore he'd get his revenge.

"You fooled me, you crook, but I won't let you get away with it. We are going to fight each other with only our fingernails as weapons, and this time the advantage will be mine." The peasant was fully aware that the Evil One had terrible claws, but he had no choice of weapons and therefore had to accept returning home without a clue how he would get out of this situation unscathed. "Let him come," his wife told him. "I'll take care of him. The day when he comes to fight you, hide, and I will talk to him."

On the day that had been set, the devil, frothing with rage, knocked at the door. "It's me, I've come to fight."

"Enter, godfather," the laborer's wife replied, "and wait for my husband. He went out to get his claws sharpened. Just look at what he did to me!"

The devil then saw a sight that made him bolt for fear of getting similar wounds,* and he never came back again.

OTTO SUTERMEISTER, *KINDER-UND
HAUSMÄRCHEN AUS DER SCHWEIZ*
(AARAU: H. R. SAUERLÄNDER, 1869), 80–83.

---

*A smutty reference to the cleft in the buttocks.

CHAPTER III

THE SWINDLED AND BATTERED DEVIL

1. The Animals and the Devil

Finland

Once upon a time there was an old man who owned three animals: a cat, a rooster, and an ox. One evening at dinner, he said to his valet, "Tomorrow morning, we must kill the cat." But after the meal, the valet advised the feline: "Flee, otherwise you will be killed tomorrow." The cat heeded this warning, and the next day, when they wished to slaughter him, he was gone without a trace.

The following night, the master of the house said, "Tomorrow morning, we must kill the rooster." The valet relayed this decision to the rooster, who left the farm in complete haste. Next it was the ox's turn to flee, and all three of them met up in the forest. They were making their way beneath the foliage when they met a wolf. "Where are you going?" they asked it.

"To find the flock. I'm going to see if I can't get a nice lamb to sink my teeth into."

"Don't go there," the others warned, "over there they will kill you. Come with us instead." The wolf accepted and they set off again as four.

A bear then crossed their path. "Where are you going?" they asked it.

"Over there, in the direction of the village, to eat some oats."

"Don't go there, something bad might happen to you, come instead with us."

The bear joined their company, and after walking for a while as five, they met a hare. They persuaded it in the same way to come with them. They came to a village and decided to go to the sauna. In front of it they found a dog who warned them: "Don't go in there, there are evil spirits inside," but the others paid him no mind. The bear lay down on the threshold, the wolf lay between the door jambs, the ox went off to look for a stable, the rooster hopped onto a perch, the cat stretched out over the wood stove, the hare lay beneath a bench, and the dog lay in the middle of the room.

The devil came and opened the door. In the blink of an eye, the wolf bit his calf, the bear struck him with its paw, the ox gored him with its horn, the rooster began crowing, the cat began meowing, the rabbit began hopping in every direction beneath the bench, and the dog ran all around the room. Terrified by this commotion, the devil fell over backwards. He barely pulled himself together, escaping the claws of his enemies, and leaped back through the door and made his way back to the forest, where he told his companions the story of what happened: "Never go to the sauna; some strangers have settled in there who are particularly violent. On the threshold, there was a tailor who stuck me with his needle, a hairy man who grappled with me and hit me, and a shoemaker who hit me with his shoe form and made me fall over backwards. On the stove someone had lit a fire and journeymen with reddened eyes were running in every direction, going from one corner to another, trying to catch me so they could beat me, but without success. When I fled, one of them was even shouting to the others, "Catch him, catch him!"

AUGUST VON LÖWIS OF MENAR,
FINNISCHE UND ESTNISCHE VOLKSMÄRCHEN
(IÉNA: EUGEN DIEDERICHS, 1922), 141–143.

Staufe 47; Gonzenbach 66; Schullerus 14.

ATU 130.

2. Johann Solves Some Riddles

Austria

Three soldiers who one day had had enough of serving left the army. They were in the company of a fourth man named Johann, whom they had tricked into accompanying them by promising him the earth. Because the four deserters couldn't afford to be noticed, they only traveled at night.

One evening, they came to the edge of a forest where they stopped to eat. After eating a few crusts of bread, they resumed their journey. Suddenly they caught a glimpse of light far off in the distance. They headed toward it and came to a house and knocked at the door. An old man (it was the devil) opened it and invited them to come inside. After three days had passed, he told them: "If you don't act as you should by tomorrow, you will belong to the devil."

Johann was very pious so he went deep into the forest, fell down on his knees, and prayed to God to help him. He then left to rejoin his comrades. All at once, he heard a strange humming in the air. He raised his eyes and saw three crows of diabolical appearance[1] perching on a tree. Curious, Johann stopped still to observe them. What was his surprise when one of them began to speak! He perked his ear and this is what he heard:[2] "Tomorrow my band will be increased by four men; for three days I have had four guests at my place to whom I'm going to ask some riddles. They must first discover that they should not sit down on a beautiful golden armchair, which in reality is a dead cat: whoever risks it shall belong to me. Next, they must not drink from a golden chalice, for that is the head of a cat; anyone who permits himself to do this will belong to me. Finally, for the last one, it's a horseshoe that will have the shape of a sword. Whosoever touches it will be mine. Aren't these fine choices?"

"Wonderful!" the other two crows replied. "We wish you good luck."

But one of them asked: "But why are you so sad, friend crow?"

"My poor princess is doing so poorly that she is confined to bed. She has a merciless duenna who is starving her. One day, without knowing it, the princess took a piece of bread from her, and when this latter entered the room, the princess threw it on the ground and trampled it underfoot. A toad that had just entered ate the bread and is crouching under the door. Since that time, the princess's condition has only grown worse. Whoever wants to rescue her will have to catch the toad and crush it underfoot; the animal will expel the bread, which must be crushed into powder and fed to the princess. Her condition will worsen initially, but then she will get better." The crows then flew away.

Johann thanked God for the way he had helped him and left to meet his comrades, who were waiting for him impatiently. However, he did not say a word to them about the events, so that he could execute his plan.

That evening, the four companions went to bed. In the morning the devil came to test them with the first object, the armchair.[3] The oldest soldier, a loafer, went to sit down in it, but Johann shouted at him just in time not to do anything, because this armchair was a cat. The devil soon returned with a chalice that the second soldier, a drunk, wanted to use immediately. "What are you going to do with that?" Johann asked him. "That's the head of an old cat." The Evil One then returned with the third object that the third companion wanted to try, but Johann warned him: "You are lost if you touch that horseshoe!" A powerful roar of thunder suddenly sounded, and our men found themselves sitting on a tree trunk.[4] This was when Johann told them of his adventure in the forest, and suggested that they make their way to the city, where the ailing princess lived. They agreed and lightheartedly set off.

After a long period of wandering, they reached the mourning city, which was all draped in black. Leaving his comrades, Johann asked to be taken to the royal palace. After much hesitation his request was granted. He was first brought before the monarch, who ordered Johann to cure his daughter and swore to have him killed if he killed her. On the other hand, if Johann saved her, he would have her hand in marriage. Refusing to be intimidated, Johann got down to work. After extracting the toad and preparing the powder, he gave it to the princess as he had learned from the crows, and went away. He returned after several hours and found the maiden completely cured. He married her, and his companions entered the king's service.

The story is done
*and the mouse has run!**

THEODOR VERNALEKEN, *KINDER-UND HAUSMÄRCHEN IN DEN ALPENLÄNDERN* (VIENNA, BRAUMILLER, 1863), 164–168.

📖 Haltrich 33.

ATU 812, BP III, 12, EM 11, 259–267.

---

*We find this ending in "Hansel and Gretel," and the comparison allows us to see that it is truncated here. It should read: "My tale is done; a mouse is running, whoever catches it can make from it a very, very large fur-lined coat" (*Mein Märchen ist aus, dort läuft eine Maus, wer sie fängt, darf sich eine große große Pelzkappe daraus machen*).

3. The Journeyman and the Devil

Norway

Once upon a time there was a journeyman who was cracking wal-
nuts as he walked along on his journey. He found one that was
wormy, and just at that moment he met the devil. "Is it true," the
lad asked, "that you can make yourself as small as you like and that
you can even slip through the eye of a needle?"

"Certainly!" replied the devil.

"Let me see by going into this walnut." The devil did just that.
Once he had gotten inside by way of the hole bored by the worm,
the journeyman stuck a wedge into it and exclaimed: "Now, I've
got you!" and put the walnut in his pocket.

After walking a while, he came to a forge, which he entered.
There he begged the smith to try and open the walnut. "That will
be a cinch," replied the man. He took his smallest hammer, placed
the walnut on the anvil, and struck it. It refused to open. The
smith then grabbed a bigger hammer, but it still was not heavy
enough. He took an even bigger one, but still to no effect. The
smith got angry and took his largest hammer. "I'm going to get
you open before I'm through," he said, striking it as hard as he
could. The walnut exploded, the roof flew off, and a large racket
was made as if the entire forge was collapsing. "A person could easily say that the devil was in this walnut!" cried the smith.

"It's quite possible," the journeyman laughed.

4. Cucendron the Giant and the Devil

Norwegian Lapland

A man had three sons, and the eldest had to leave in search of
work. He put together some provisions for the journey and left.

After traveling a ways, he sat down to have lunch. While he was eating, an axe, an auger, a plane, and all sorts of tools flew up to him, all asking for a little food, but he didn't give them the smallest crumb. Once he was replete, he resumed his journey and came to a castle. "Where are you going?" asked the king.

"I'm looking for a job," he replied.

"I can offer you one," the sovereign said. "In my garden grows a tree covered with gold leaves. If you are able to spend a single night guarding it, you shall have my daughter and half of my kingdom."

When night fell, the son made his way to the garden, where he sat down next to the tree and watched the leaves open and grow. They had almost completed their growth when he became extremely drowsy and was powerless to resist. He soon fell into a deep sleep. When he awoke, the gold leaves had disappeared, and that morning, when the king asked him if he had kept guard, he could only reply: "No, I was not able to." The monarch then ordered his execution.

His younger brother decided to leave home, and with a heavy heart his father gave him his blessing. The young man then prepared provisions for his journey and set off. The same thing that befell his brother befell him: he fell asleep and was punished in the same way.

The youngest brother, whom his brothers called Scabby* or Cucendron,† decided that he, too, wanted to leave to seek his fortune. His father opposed his wish, as he believed his fate would be worse anywhere else but home. The boy persisted in his desires and his father eventually surrendered, but only gave him a few provisions. The lad took his satchel in one hand, and a large glove in the other, and set off.

After walking for a good while, he sat down to have lunch. Suddenly an axe, an auger, a plane, and all sorts of other tools

---

*Knöbba.

†Gudnavirus.

showed up to beg some food from him, and he gave a few crumbs from the little he had to each of them. He then got up, resumed his journey, and came to the royal castle. "Where are you going?" the sovereign asked him.

"I'm looking to enter the service of anyone who would like to do well by me," he replied.

"I can hire you."

"What will I have to do?"

"In my garden stands a tree with leaves of gold. If you are capable of guarding it for a single night, you shall have my daughter and half of my kingdom."

"I'm going to take my chances."

At dusk, he was taken to the tree, and because he was small, someone sat him on one of the lower branches. When darkness fell, the leaves began to grow, but the more they grew, the sleepier the lad became. He forced his eyes to stay open and somehow managed to stay awake. Finally, even though slumber was still threatening to carry him off, he heard a horrible din in the air and it scared him so much that he woke up completely. His wide-open eyes fell upon two very ugly, big, strapping men arriving in a storm. One was a giant and the other was the devil, but they only had one eye between the two of them. "Check to see if anyone is guarding the tree," said the giant to the devil, who was holding the eye.

"Oh fie!" the devil exclaimed. "We will take the leaves; watcher or not, we have never run into any problem when picking them."

"Fine, climb the tree then," said the giant.

"No, it's you who climbs. I'm going to give you the eye." The giant climbed up and reached for the eye.

The devil held it out to him, but at that very moment the boy grabbed it and slipped it into his glove. "Give me the eye," the giant said.

"But you already got it, idiot!" In a rage, the giant leapt on the devil, and they grappled until both fell down dead.

When day broke, the lad went to find the king. "How did everything go? Did you keep watch?" the sovereign asked.

"Of course," the boy replied.

The king sent his men to verify, and they returned to say the boy was speaking the truth: the tree was covered with the most beautiful gold leaves. "Am I going to marry your daughter?" the boy asked.

"Not yet."

"What must I do to win her?"

"If you build a boat in one night and bring it to me, you shall have my daughter."

"That's completely impossible! How could I build a boat in a single night and bring it here? Nonetheless, I am going to try."

When night fell, he left with his axe and once in the forest, stuck it in a tree while saying loudly: "Now you tools that I fed, come forth quickly and craft a boat that you shall place in front of the king's gate!" Upon this an intense burst of activity got underway: the sound of hammering, sawing, and planing could be heard in every direction; all the tools were getting down to work. The boy sat down to watch them. In no time at all, a ship appeared that kept getting bigger and bigger until it was completely finished. He climbed on board immediately and left.

While on his way, he met a man who was gnawing on some bones. As the boat passed near him, he asked: "What are you doing?"

"I've been eating bones all my life," the man replied, "without ever being able to satisfy my hunger."

"Climb onto my boat, you will get marrow bones!" The man obliged, and this is how the boy made a friend.

A little later, they passed by a man sucking on a piece of ice. "What are you doing?" he asked.

"I've sucked on ice all my life, but my thirst has never been quenched."

"Sail with us and it shall be!" This is how the boy gained a new companion.

They set off again and spotted another man who was lifting one leg, then lifting the other, without advancing. "What are you doing?"

"All my life I've been trying to start walking, but I am always stuck in the same place."

"Climb aboard, and you will finally move forward!" said the boy, who now had three comrades.

They continued their journey and saw someone aiming without firing. "What are you doing?" the boy asked him.

"For all my life I've been able to aim, but I've never succeeded in getting any farther."

"Get on board, and it will finally work!" The other obliged and the boy now had a crew at his disposal.

He continued his journey and by morning had reached the palace. Once there, he went in to fetch the king. "So is the boat finished?" the king asked him.

"Of course!"

The monarch went outside to check and found it ready to sail. "Will you give me your daughter, now?"

"Not yet."

"Why?"

"Tonight, go fetch the golden chalice that belongs to my neighbor king, and place it on my table. Then you shall have my daughter."

"That's impossible! How could I get there in a single night and be back by tomorrow morning?"

"That's your business."

"I'm going to try," replied the boy. He went in search of the man who took great strides and told him: "Stout companion! If never before were you able to make a single step, now's the time. Walk until you reach the palace of the neighboring king, take his gold cup, and bring it back tomorrow morning." The man left, but as dawn began to break, he still had not returned.

"Brave marksman," said the lad, "fire a shot into the sole of the walker's foot so he speeds up."

While on his journey back, the walker had met a young woman and stopped. But when the marksman did what he had been asked, the walker remembered his mission and arrived back before it was completely light out. The boy took the chalice to the king and placed it on his table. "Am I going to get your daughter now?"

"Yes," the monarch replied, and the wedding was performed. Me, I left again.

JOSEF CARL POESTION, *LAPPLÄNDISCHE MÄRCHEN,*
VOLKSSAGEN, RÄTHSEL UND SPRICHWÖRTER
(VIENNA: VERLAG VON CARL GEROLDS SOHN, 1886), 104–110.

ATU 513 B.

5. The Captain and the Old Erik

Norway

Once upon a time there was a captain whose every undertaking succeeded in a way no one could understand. No one else was entrusted with such profitable cargos, and no one else made as much money, for blessings seemed to shower on this lucky captain from every side. No one had as much talent as he did for making these kinds of voyages because, wherever he went, the wind was always with him. It was even said that by simply turning his hat, he directed the wind in the direction he wanted.

For many years he traveled, trading for wood with China for three years and making money as easily as if he were harvesting grass. One day, he was returning home by the North Sea, sailing at top speed as if he had stolen the boat and all its merchandise.

But the one who wanted to catch him was going even faster. It was Gamle Erik,* with whom he'd signed a contract, and as one can imagine, today was the day it came due. He could expect that Gamle Erik would come to personally fetch him at the right time.

Fine! The captain stepped out of the deckhouse and climbed to the bridge, then called the carpenter and other members of his crew. There and then he ordered them to go down into the hold to bore two holes at the bottom of the boat. Once this was done, they would have to remove the pumps from their usual location and hermetically seal the holes with them, so that seawater would rise into the pumps.

The crew was astounded and thought that this was a madman's work, but they obeyed their captain. They pierced two holes at the bottom of the hull, and set the pumps over them so tightly that not a single drop of water could enter the ship's hold. But in the pumps the water had risen seven feet.

The crew had just tossed wood shavings overboard when Gamle Eric climbed aboard in a fierce gust of wind and grabbed the captain by the throat. "Not so fast! There is no need to rush," said the captain, defending himself. With the help of a marlin-spike, he loosened the claws the devil had grabbed him with.

"Wasn't it part of our agreement that you will keep this vessel dry and watertight?" the captain asked. "Well, then, measure the water in the pumps: it has risen seven feet. Pump, you devil that you are, and empty the water from the boat! Then you can take me if you wish."

The devil was too stupid not to be taken in. He toiled and pumped; such a torrent of sweat flowed down his back that it could turn a water wheel. He pumped the water out of the hold, spilling it into the North Sea, but it just came back. Finally, exhausted by this labor and in a very bad mood, he left to take a

---

*One of the devil's names in Norway: the Old-Erik; variant: Gammelerik, Gamleeirik. In England this is Old Nick.

Illustration by Nils Wiwel
(1857–1914) for Asbjørnsen's
story, "Skipperen og
Gamle-Erik."

rest at his grandmother's house. As for the captain, the devil let
him sail as long as he wanted, and if he is not dead, he may still be
voyaging, turning the wind in the direction he wishes with his hat.

P. C. Asbjørnsen & Jørgen Moe, *Eventyr*
(Oslo: Gyldendal Norsk Forlag, 1928), n 81.

6. The Cunning Schoolteacher and the Devil

Transylvania

One day a schoolteacher went to help a shepherd harvest his hay with
a large pitchfork—as was once customary to do here and there—
and brought a piece of bread and a small hunk of cheese with him
to serve as his meal. His path took him across the devil's pasture,
where suddenly he saw that very individual carrying on his back a
buffalo-hide wineskin, which he wanted to fill with water. "Stop!"
the devil yelled at the schoolteacher. "I've got you!" The devil threw
down his wineskin and tried to grab him, but the teacher took out

his cheese and squeezed until water leaked from it, then threw it at the devil. "Look! I will squeeze you like this rock until your blood spills out if you merely dare to touch me!" In terror, the devil ran off, leaving his wineskin behind. As he ran away, he shouted: "I met a man so strong that he was able to squeeze water out of a rock!" The other demons sent him to hire the man to be a water-bearer. He therefore returned to the pasture, and offered the schoolteacher a job. Our hero accepted because this would give him an opportunity to visit hell. As soon as he arrived, he was given the order to fill a large wineskin with water, but it was so heavy that even empty he could not lift it. He then thought of a ruse: he took a spade and a pickax, and acted as if he were about to leave.

"Where are you going with those tools?"

"I'm going to dig up the spring and bring it back here so I will not have to constantly go there." Fearing that hell would be flooded, and their fires extinguished, the devils grew scared. "Leave it be, we will go fetch our own water," they told him.

Then they wanted him to go into the forest to take down an oak tree and bring it back to them. The schoolteacher gave it some thought: "This is what they are going to see!" He conceived of a new strategy. He picked up a large rope and started on his way. "What are you going to do with that rope?" the devils asked him.

"Tie all the trees together, tear them down, and bring them back so I don't have to return to the woods too often."

Terrified by the man's monstrous strength, they feared that if he brought back the entire forest, hell would burn it all at once and then, later, they would die from the cold. "Don't speak of it anymore, we will go fetch our wood ourselves."

They then decided to rid themselves of this dangerous man and told him: "We are ready to pay you your salary on the condition that you leave." The schoolteacher accepted, but demanded that one of the devils carry the sack of gold to his house personally. None of them wished to take such a risk, but one finally agreed to do it. When they arrived within sight of the school, the teacher's children were looking out the window. Their father made a sign to them and they all began shouting as one: "Me too, I want to eat some devil, me too, I want to eat some devil." On hearing these words, the devil hurled the sack to the ground and bolted back to hell as fast as he could with nary a backward glance.

But one of his sons, a hearty, swaggering devil who had just returned from abroad, said he was ready to fearlessly take on any man. His father and his assistants asked him to go to the schoolteacher's house and bring back the bag of gold. As soon as he was ready he set out, and when he arrived, he shouted: "Either you give me the bag or you will have to contend with me!" Laughing, the teacher replied: "You can always run away! But I would not be averse to fighting with you. What should we start with?"

"Wrestling," replied the devil.

"Ah, I would be too scared of crushing your bones! But I have an old grandfather here who is still strong enough to defeat you." He then released a bear that hurled itself on the devil, grabbed him with its paws, and squeezed him so hard that he howled: "Ow, ow, ow, stop!" Teasing him, the schoolteacher then said, "Perhaps wrestling is not your strong suit? Choose something else."

"Let's compete at racing!"

"I would be dishonored if I accepted this challenge, but I have a grandson here who will beat you." He then let loose a hare, who disappeared from sight as quickly as an arrow. The devil soon returned, all out of breath and half dead. "You don't really run all that well," the schoolteacher mocked him. "Perhaps you are better in some other discipline?"

"Now we are going to see who can throw the highest," replied the furious devil in a rage. He took an enormous long-handled smith's hammer,* and threw it so high that it took seven hours to

---

*A blacksmithing hammer with a long handle.

fall back to earth. He then handed it to the teacher saying: "Now, show us what you can do." Seeing that he could not even lift it, he answered, "If I throw it, it will not fall back again, because I have a brother-in-law who is a blacksmith. He will snag the hammer so he can use it to make carpenter's nails while we wait for it in vain. I'm going to go fetch a stone that I will throw." He let a chaffinch out of its cage. Thrilled to be free, the bird soared off. The teacher had positioned the devil so that he was facing the sun so squarely that he never noticed that the bird had vanished in the sky. "It will take seven days for the stone to fall back to earth. Do you want to wait so long?" the schoolteacher asked him.

"Oh no," the devil shot back. Half-blinded by the sun, he had had enough.

"Hee hee," the schoolteacher teased him, "you other devils are not so gifted. You don't know how to wrestle, run, or throw something in the air. Just what are you good at?"

"Let's see how you measure up at cracking a whip," the other replied, angry and annoyed.

He picked up a whip and cracked it so terribly that it gashed the teacher's belly and he almost fainted from the blow. However, he pulled himself together and said: "I feel very worried for you, let me blindfold you because I'm going to crack my whip so violently that it will thunder and cause lightning flashes that could blind you." The teacher took his bread slicer* and struck the devil's eyes with it so forcefully that he believed he had lost them. "Stop!" he groaned.

"I really wonder if there is any discipline in which you excel." Boiling with rage, the devil replied, "Let's meet head-to-head with quarter staffs!"

"That suits me!" And the teacher gave him a long iron bar, while he took a short one for himself. The teacher was able to get

---

*Paluckesklüppel. Palukes is a Wallachian word of Hungarian origin.

in close to his adversary and battered him with countless blows so that he was covered with bruises, because, at a disadvantage because of his weapon's length, the devil could not riposte. "Let's swap weapons then!" the latter said.

"Gladly, but you are so pitiable that I'm going to grant you an advantage: slip into the pig sty, where you will be protected while I remain outside to fight. The devil agreed, took the short bar, and entered the pig sty. With his long iron bar the schoolteacher struck him so mercilessly that he pierced his chest, while the devil was unable to land a single blow with his short rod. "Enough, enough!" the teacher howled when he saw blood streaming down on all sides. "Let no one come and try to tell me that a devil is superior to even the most pathetic man. Haven't you now proven that you are completely incapable of doing anything well, unless you wish to try something else?" Howling in pain and rage, the devil shouted: "Yes, yes, let's have a scratching contest!" He then scratched the schoolteacher down to the bone, causing a jet of blood to gush out. "Wait for me to go get my nails," said the teacher, "I always take them off when I don't need them. He brought back two carding combs and pitilessly carved such deep furrows in his adversary's skin that the latter, yowling in pain, shouted: "Stop, you are wounding me too deeply!"

"I would really be ashamed to continue fighting with you," said the teacher, "and I think that this is the end of your boasting."

Frothing with rage, the demon replied: "For the last test, let's have a farting contest." The devil than let off one that was so potent it plastered the schoolteacher against the ceiling. "What are you doing up there?" asked the devil.

"I'm plugging up the cracks and holes so that you cannot get out when I break wind; it will shatter you against the ceiling."

All the hair on the devil's head stood up in fright, and not waiting another instant, he took to his heels and ran straight back to hell.

Since that time, the devils have left the schoolteacher in peace, but some robbers have likely stolen his bag of gold, for he is as poor as Job. Some say that it was Ion the Strong or the tailor Zwirn* that actually defeated the devil in the seven arts,† but this is false: the schoolteacher has told this story many times himself, so it must therefore be him.

Josef Haltrich, *Deutsche Volksmärchen aus dem*
Sachsenlande in Siebenbür- gen
(Vienna: Verlag von Carl Graeser,
Julius Springer, 1856), 161–167.
ATU 1045, 1060, 1071, 1083, 1095.

7. The King's Son and the Devil's Daughter

Transylvania

Once upon a time there was a king who, during a war, had lost every battle one after another. His armies had been annihilated and he was so desperate that he was thinking of putting an end to his days. Suddenly a man appeared before him and said: "I know your problem. Courage, I will help you if you promise to give me the new thing that just entered your house. At the end of three times seven years, I will return to collect what's owed me." The king didn't grasp what had happened to him, and thought the stranger was talking about a new rope—*en noa sil,* "a new soul," is said the same as "a new rope" in Saxon—and accepted such a modest price without hesitation. "You have plenty in your storeroom," he said to himself.

The sovereign had long been without any descendants, but while he had been at war a son had been born to him that he knew

---

*Names of two very popular folktale heroes.
†Allusion to the seven liberal arts (*die sieben freien Künste*).

naught of. However, the stranger did know, because he was the supreme devil. As soon as the monarch had agreed to his bargain, the devil stepped away a short distance, took an iron whip with four tails, and cracked it in each of the four directions. And just look! Immediately warriors flooded in from all sides in large numbers, and at their head the sovereign won battle after battle. His martial success was such that in a very short time his enemy was suing for peace.

He returned to his kingdom, and the joy he gained from his victory knew no bounds when he learned that a son and successor had been born to him. He viewed himself as the happiest of men because, on the one hand, he was a powerful king who was feared and loved by his subjects, and, on the other, he had a son who was perfect in every way, who would soon grow in strength and beauty.

Almost three times seven years since the great war had passed and the king had completely forgotten his promise when, one day, the stranger suddenly reappeared, dressed as he had been before. He had come to claim, in accordance with the contract, *en noa sil*. Wishing to show his full gratitude, the monarch had the longest and newest rope in his possession brought forth, but the stranger refused it, smiling disdainfully and shouting: "It's a new soul that I requested—your son who was born at that very moment. Now he belongs to me and must follow me into my kingdom at once!" Horrified, the king tore his hair, rent his garments, wrung his hands, and came close to dying from his pain, but in vain. Then his son, of a pure and innocent heart, consoled him. "Don't act so, father. This horrible prince of hell will not be able to do anything to me." In a rage, the devil exclaimed: "Wait and see, you model of virtue, you will pay for this!" He seized the son and carried him through the air until they reached hell.

The entire kingdom went into mourning. Every home was draped in black crepe, and the king, lost in his grief, locked himself in his palace—a dead man among the living.

Now back in his kingdom with the king's son, the prince of hell showed him the infernal furnace, telling him that they were going to heat it seven times hotter and that he would be cast into it in the morning if he was not able to do as he was ordered during the night.

There was a pond of monstrous size very close by. The devil ordered the prince to drain it dry during the night and transform it into a large meadow, which he would then harvest for hay. He would then have to bale it so that all he needed to do the next day was bring it in. There and then the devil locked the young man in a room and left him alone. Sad and overwhelmed, he readied himself to face death, for carrying off this undertaking successfully was unthinkable. Suddenly, the door opened and the devil's daughter entered to bring the king's son his lunch. Seeing this handsome lad weeping stirred something in her heart. She took pity on him and told him: "Eat, drink, and take courage. I am going to arrange matters so that everything my father has ordered you to do will be achieved. You may show a tranquil face tomorrow." With these words she left, but the prince remained sad. During the night, the daughter of the devil rose quietly from her bed, went to her father's bed, and plugged his ears. She then took his whip with the four tails, left, and cracked it toward each of the four directions. This awoke a thousand echoes that shook the entire infernal empire. The air bustled with noise everywhere as infernal spirits rushed to her, asking, "What is your command?" A violent hubbub resounded for a moment, similar to a raging storm, along with some violent knocks, before calm was restored. To his great surprise and immense joy, when the prince looked out his window early in the morning he saw a pile of hay bales where the pond had once been. He took heart at the sight and felt reassured.

Once she had finished, the devil's daughter removed her father's earplugs and put his whip back in its place. When he awoke, he wickedly rejoiced in anticipation of watching the prince burn in his fire. So you can imagine his surprise when he stepped outside and saw that the impossible task had been accomplished. Even angrier than the day before, he sought out the young man and told him: "You succeeded this time, but tomorrow you will get a taste of my furnace! See that large forest on the mountain! You have to chop it all down tonight and stack up all the wood, so that we can bring it in tomorrow. In place of the forest, you have to make vines grow, and their grapes must be ripe enough to be harvested." He shut the door, leaving the prince to abandon himself once more to despair, for he thought that the task was impossible. The devil's daughter then entered with his meal, was informed about her father's latest command, and consoled him. Restored to calm, he took new heart. Over the course of the night, the devil's daughter did the same as she had the previous night. That morning, the devil, curious to learn if the stupid mortal had again succeeded, saw to his great amazement that this was indeed the case. His fury reached its peak! "You have been successful again this time. Now let's see if your cleverness can save you a third time. During the night, you will have to build a church out of sand, complete with dome and cross, and it must be solid and resistant." Then the devil shut the door and left, and the dismayed prince felt discouragement sinking its claws into him again.

When the devil's daughter brought him his meal, he told her of his distress and described what his new task consisted of. "This is a difficult thing," she said, "and I fear I might fail. But I'm going to try. Don't close your eyes at all tonight, so that you may hear me when I call you." At midnight, after plugging her father's ears, the devil's daughter made use of his whip. Immediately busy servitors showed up and asked for their orders. When she explained what she needed them to do, they exclaimed in great fear: "Build a church! Not now, not later! Not even one in stone or iron, not to mention sand!" But the devil's daughter sternly ordered them to get to work. They went off and began working, but were soon covered in sweat, because the sand just flowed through their fingers and the work did not advance. Several times they had erected half the church before it collapsed again. Once they were almost finished, and even the dome had been set up. All that was missing was the cross. But when the devils tried to place it on the top, the entire edifice crumbled. When the devil's daughter saw that the work was futile and the time was almost up, she sent the devils away and ran to the prince's window shouting: "Get up! Get up! There is still time for me to rescue you if you want to be saved. I am going to transform into a white horse. Mount it and I will carry you." No sooner said than done, and off they fled at a triple gallop.

When the devil woke up, everything seemed unnaturally silent. He sought to grab his whip to wake up his folk, but it wasn't in its place. He opened his mouth and all hell echoed with his howls. His ears became unclogged and he realized that the entire household was already hard at work. He thought of the prince and made his way to his chamber. Upon entering he found the door already opened and the young man absent. He went in search of his whip, which he finally found in a corner. He cracked it to the four winds, and all the devils of his kingdom appeared. "What is your command for us? We have worked all night, can't you give us a little time to rest?"

"Who gave you those orders?"

"Your daughter."

"My daughter!" yelled the horrified prince of hell. "She has displayed compassion; now everything is clear to me. She plugged my ears, had the work performed by using my power for the love of this wretch, and now she has left with him. Wait and see, I will soon catch them!" He then soared off in search of the fugitives, and soon spotted the white horse and its rider. Diving toward the ground, he shouted to his devils: "Hurry up and bring me back the white horse and its rider, dead or alive!" The sky immediately grew dark with flying demons. Hearing this humming from afar, the horse asked her rider: "What do you see behind us?"

"A black cloud."

"That's the troop of my father pursuing us. We are lost if you don't do exactly as I say. I am going to transform into a church and you into a priest. Stand in front of the altar and sing without stopping, even if anyone asks you a question."

The prince promised to obey. As they drew near, the demons came to a halt in amazement at the sight of this large church. But even though all the doors were open, they could not cross through them no mater how hard they tried. The prince changed into a priest and stood near the altar, chanting: "Lord, be with us, Lord, protect us!" The devils listened to this strange singing for a long time, but because the officiating figure never stopped, they couldn't ask him if he had seen a white horse and rider. He didn't miss a beat, and continued to chant, so they resumed their journey to the edge of the infernal kingdom without ever catching a glimpse of either the rider or his mount. In the evening, when they returned empty-handed, the old devil spit flames in his anger.

He flew in pursuit of the fugitives the next day, and spotted the church in the distance. He could hear the murmur of the chant, which caused him to shudder. "It's them," he told himself. "Just wait and see, you can't fool me!" He assembled an even larger troop than the first one and yelled: "Charge into the church and destroy it from top to bottom. Bring me back a stone from it as well as the priest, dead or alive!" The demons soared off in the blink of an eye, but in the meantime the devil's daughter and the prince had resumed their earlier forms and fled. A short time later they heard a whistling and humming behind them.

"What do you see?" the horse asked.

"A cloud that is even larger and more frightening than the first one!"

"That's my father's new troop. Do exactly what I tell you to do or we are lost. I am going to transform myself into an alder tree and you into a little golden bird. Don't stop singing because you let yourself get alarmed or scared."

The infernal troop had almost caught up to them in a place that was just about seven hundred leagues from where the church had stood, but they found no trace of the church, the priest, the white horse, or the prince. When the troop came to the foot of the alder, they stopped in amazement to look at the tree and the bird that sang without ceasing: "Don't have any fear of me, don't have any fear of me."

"If only the bird would shut up," the devils said, "so that we could ask about the church, the priest, the white horse, and the prince." But the bird never stopped singing. The devils again went to the farthest end of the kingdom, and again returned that evening in failure. The old devil vomited torrents of flame in anger, and the next day set off himself in pursuit of the fugitives.

He caught a glimpse of the alder tree and the bird whose song caused him to shudder. "Aha, you won't escape me!" He told the immense troop he had assembled: "Hurry forth, cut down the alder tree and bring me back a shaving of its wood, and catch the bird and bring it back to me, dead or alive!" The devils immediately flew off, but in the meantime the alder and the bird had turned back into a horse and rider and already traveled another seven hundred leagues. When she heard the throbbing noise, the white horse asked: "What do you see behind you?"

"A black cloud that is even more frightening than the previous ones."

"It's my father's troop. Do exactly what I tell you or otherwise we are lost. I am going to transform into a rice paddy and change you into a quail. Travel across the paddy in every direction without stopping your singing, and don't let yourself be interrupted by any question."

The prince promised. The infernal army drew near, looking in every direction without seeing a church, priest, alder, or bird, not to mention a white horse and its rider. When they saw the rice paddy, they came to a halt in amazement, watching the comings and going of the quail and listening to its song: "God be with us, may He be with us."

"If only that bird would stop so we can question it," they said, but the bird continued and they had to return empty-handed. The devil now boiled over in fury and soared off. He caught sight of the rice paddy and the bird, and exclaimed: "You are in my power. Press on to banish this rice paddy and catch the quail," he told his servitors.

"Wait! This time I have to pursue them myself, for if they travel four times seven hundred leagues, I will have no more power and they will be able to mock me." The devil's daughter and the prince had already covered a good distance. They needed to only travel another seven hundred leagues to get out of hell. They then heard an impressive din behind them. The horse asked its rider, "What do you see behind us?"

"A black dot in the sky, blacker than night, from which flashes of fire are shooting."

"Oh woe, that's my father! We are lost if you don't obey me to the letter. I am going to transform myself into a large pond of milk and change you into a duck. Always swim in the center of the pond without showing your head, so that nothing can encompass you! Don't take your head out of the milk, and don't swim toward the bank," she said, and the prince promised.

The devil had soon reached the edge of the pond. But he could do nothing against them as long as the duck was not in his power, because it was swimming in the middle of the pond. He was too far away for him to reach it. He could not swim out to him, because devils drown in pure milk. There was only one solution: lure the duck. "Little duck, why are you swimming in the middle of the pond? Look around you. How fine it is where I am!" But the duckling did not look or listen. However, he felt the desire to pull

his head out of the milk at least once. Because the Tempter continued his game, the duckling dared a quick glance. Immediately the
Evil One stole his sight, and he found that he was blind. The milk
pond began to turn cloudy and ferment, and a plaintive voice made
itself heard by the duck: "Oh woe, what have you done?" The devil's
daughter promised herself that she would never allow herself to be
seduced, while her father danced with evil joy on the bank, howling
"Aha, I will have you soon!" And he tried to swim out to the duck
to grab it. Because he started sinking, he quickly turned back. For
a long time he tried to entice the duck to come to the bank, but the
bird remained still, with its head plunged into the milk, mocking
the Evil One. Furious and hopping up and down with impatience,
the devil suddenly transformed into a pelican and swallowed the
milk pond with the duck. Stumbling, he turned around. A voice
emerging from the milk told the duck: "All is going to be well now,"
and the milk began fermenting and boiling. The devil felt heavier
and heavier and, feeling oppressed, could only move with difficulty.
"If only I was at home," he sighed, but this did no good. The boiling
milk had caused him to swell, and he started wobbling. Suddenly an
enormous noise was heard as he exploded and died. The prince and
the devil's daughter appeared in the splendor of their young beauty.

The prince took the devil's daughter to his father's kingdom,
where they arrived seven days after the young man had been
abducted. Cries of joy echoed throughout the entire land. The
dark funeral drapes were taken down, and rice and flowers were
strewn on their path. The old sovereign went out to meet them to
the sound of drums and trumpets. A splendid wedding was celebrated, after which the king handed power over to his son. The
new king ruled as wisely and fairly as his father, and if he hasn't
died in the meantime, he is still ruling today.

Josef Haltrich, <i>Deutsche Volksmärchen aus
dem Sachsenlande in Sibenbürgen</i>
(Berlin: Julius Springer, 1856), 151–183.

📖 In story type ATU 313 C we can find a variant of this one; cf. Espinosa, Aurelio, *Cuentos populares de Castilla y León* (Madrid, 1987), vol. 1, 143–47.

ATU 313 A, EM 9, COL. 13–19, MLEX 62–66.

8. The Man and the Devil

Russia

A man went hunting in the forest. The devil saw him and asked: "What are you doing here?"

"I have come to go hunting," the man replied.

"You have not taken anything?"

"Nothing!"

"Come, let's go hunt, take this path and I will take the other," and they separated.

After walking a short while, the hunter found a reindeer antler that he hung at his belt. The devil killed a reindeer, hurled it over his shoulders, and met up with the man again. He asked him: "My friend, you did not get anything?"

"I killed a reindeer that I tied to my belt, but it came off. I wasn't paying attention; only the antler has remained."

"Very well, my friend, one single reindeer should be enough for the two of us," and he carried the animal and the man to his place.

They cooked it, ate it, and then went to bed. The Evil One invited the man to take the bed near the window, the bed over which a millstone was hanging. The man placed his clothes on the bed, and then went to sleep in front of the stove. The devil let the millstone fall on what he believed to be his guest. In the morning he went in and asked, "My friend, did you sleep well?"

"Without any problem!"

The next evening, the devil offered the same bed, but our

hero placed a bundle of hemp on it, then left and took up watch in front of the window. The One-Eyed One (in other words, the devil) entered, chewed on it—cratch, cratch—then tossed it aside. The man then went back to his place. In the morning the Evil One entered and asked: "My friend, did you sleep well?"

"It seems that I was bitten by lice or fleas," he replied.

The devil went to see his mother and told her: "It's miraculous, Mother: I really chewed him up good, and he says it was only lice or fleas that bit him."

For the third time, the devil offered him the same place. Our hero got up and filled the bed with tiles, then went to lie down in front of the stove. The One-Eyed One entered and began chewing the tiles—criss, criss—and even broke a tooth. He told his mother: "It's magnificent, Mother, he has to be dead now!" In the morning the devil entered and asked the man: "My friend, did you sleep well?"

"I don't know if I was bitten by lice or fleas," he replied.

With that, the Evil One ordered the man to go home. "Out of the question!" his guest replied. The devil sent him back home after giving him a chest full of money, and as he was incapable of carrying it, it was the devil himself who bore it on his shoulders all the way to their destination. It is said that this man became very rich.

YRJÖ, WODTJACKISCHE* SPRACHPROBEN,
VOL. 2: SPRICHWÖRTER, RÄTSEL, MÄRCHEN,
SAGEN UND ERZÄHLUNGEN (HELSINGFORS, 1893-1901), 62–65.

9. The Black School

Denmark

Once, in the same city there lived a rich man with two sons and a poor man who had an only child. The three boys went to the same

---

*The votjak oudmourte is spoken in Russia and is part of the languages spoken in the Urals.

school and were very good friends. The poor lad had the keenest wit and was very hardworking, and always helped the others learn their lessons so they wouldn't fall behind. The boys grew older, and at the time of their confirmation, the rich boys begged their parents to buy their friend the same outfit as theirs. They agreed, and when his time came to learn a trade, his friends planned to continue their studies. The rich boys told their parents, "We will not succeed if he is not with us, because we can't do without his help." Their parents consented to letting the boy study with their sons.

The three boys continued to study together, as was their custom. Their friendship was close and as the poor boy displayed the best aptitude and highest diligence, he continued to help his two comrades. They became university students together and lived together, the two rich sons sharing their money so that their friend could continue his studies in return for his help with theirs. After three years, they had learned all there was to learn at the university they were attending.

Nonetheless, there remained a great many things to discover. They all agreed they should stay together and dedicate themselves to learning what they did not yet know, and this is how they decided to study at the black school. Despite their father's summons to return home, they disobeyed him because they still had some money left, and with their friend moved to a city where teachers of the occult sciences could be found.

After making inquiries about who was the most erudite teacher there, they paid him a visit to see if he would accept them as students. "It's possible," he told them. "You could live at my place and in a year I will have taught you all I know. But you will have to sign a pact with me: When the year is over, I will ask you three questions. If you give me the right answers, you will be freed of any further obligation and will not have to pay me a cent. But the one who cannot answer the question I pose will belong to me for the rest of his natural life, and I can make whatever use I please of him." Feeling that they were already well-educated and had an entre year to perfect their knowledge, the three students believed they would be able to answer the questions and therefore signed his agreement. They then moved in with their teacher, an astounding man. He was small and always dressed in grey. His nose was like an eagle's beak and he had two deep-set red eyes. He had a large mouth that was always open in a fixed smile and two ears that resembled goat horns. He limped because he had a lame foot, which is likely why he was never seen to leave his house. The three students were treated well; an old woman took care of them as well as the house. She seemed to be deaf and mute, and among themselves they called her the devil's great-grandmother, which was taken rather well by the house's other occupant.

The teacher instructed them every day and gave them many strange books to read, and, as was usually the case, the poor man's son studied from morning to night. However, his companions soon wearied of this routine. Because a large city was just outside the door, with all its many distractions and temptations, they spent the bulk of their time enjoying all it had to offer, and led a dissolute life. Once their money was spent, they borrowed from whomever they could, their only concern being to spend their days as quickly and pleasantly as possible.

Time passed and their year of apprenticeship neared its end. They began to think about what they had signed concerning the questions they would have to answer if they did not want to belong to the man for the rest of their lives. The more they saw of him, the less they wished to fall under his power. They realized that it would be easy for him to ask questions that they would be incapable of answering. Even the poor man's son, although he had worked as hard as he could, did not enjoy any peace of mind when contemplating the upcoming exam. So it was far worse for his companions who had spent more time contemplating the bottoms of their glasses than their books.

On the eve of the last day, the poor student went to a church as he had always done. He was so preoccupied that he heard nothing of the sermon or songs. As he was leaving, he met a beautiful old woman who was asking for alms. He plunged his hand into his pocket, where he found only a few pennies,* but he gave her what he had. "Take it all, I don't need it anymore," he said.

"It's easy to see that something is weighing on your mind," she said. "Confide your cares to me, maybe I can offer you some good advice." Initially he refused: "What good would it do for me to reveal it to you?"

"I might be able to help you. I have already helped more than one person who put their trust in me." So he told her everything, how he and his comrades had studied at the house of a certain teacher, and how, the next day, they would have to answer his three questions or belong to him forever, and how this was making him very anxious. "You have every reason to be anxious," the woman replied, "for you have been studying with the devil in person. I'm going to give you some advice that will help all of you. Late tonight, take a spade and go to the cemetery, where you will cut out a piece of turf around an ell† in size. This you will carry to the hill north of the city where the gallows are erected. In the south slope of this hill you will dig a hole in the ground large enough for you to fit inside. Next you will get inside the hole and place the piece of sod you cut on top of you. You must have done all this before midnight. Wait quietly for an hour and you will then learn all that you need to know."

The student followed her suggestions and before midnight he was hidden in his hole. Then out of both the east and west some crows arrived. They began to chat, and he knew enough to understand their language. "Where is he, where is he?" they were saying. Finally a crow flew in from the south to join them. They

---

*Skillinger, which corresponds to the French sou or English penny.
†Approximately 18 inches.

chatted, debated, screeched, and squawked. The last one to arrive was in reality his teacher, who had an appointment with a group of his fellows, and the boy heard him say, "Tomorrow, the three students will be ours."

"What questions are you going to ask them?" asked a voice. The teacher revealed the three questions the unfortunate students would have to answer, questions which were naturally impossible to answer, so impossible that he was sure he would get all three of them. The crows snickered, chatted, and squawked some more before going their own ways.

Once they had gone far enough, the boy returned home and he slept as he had not been able the whole week. In the morning, after first consulting together in secret, the three of them all had lunch with their teacher. The meal was more generous than usual, as they had to pass their exam, and the time so long awaited by their teacher soon arrived. On the table they saw a scarlet blanket on which a piece of dazzling white linen, carved crystal goblets, and a finely engraved silver tray had been placed. After the meal, the teacher turned to the eldest of the two rich boys and said: "With all you studied and learned, it's not too much to ask you to tell me what the blanket you see on the table is made of."

"It's an old horse hide that you took from a slaughterhouse,"* he replied, and immediately they could all see that this was perfectly accurate. The deep-set red eyes of their teacher sank even deeper and he squinted at them abominably. However he calmly said, "So it is!"

Then turning to his younger brother, he asked him: "And what are those goblets from which you drank made of?"

"They are nothing but old pot shards," he replied, and they could all see that this was true. Unable to stay still any longer, the teacher immediately hobbled over to the son of the poor man,

---

*The devil uses his artifices here to create praestigia.

grabbed him by the arm so violently that it left bruises, and asked him in a trembling voice: "According to you, what is this tray set in the middle of the table?"

"It's an old horse skull," replied the student, and immediately they all saw him stare at them through empty eye sockets. "Get out!" the teacher shouted. "I will mark the last one to leave in such a way that he will never forget it!"

The poor student pushed the other two out in front of him and they charged toward the door. Following them, he took off the garter from his right leg and gave it a human appearance. He then leaped to the door. The teacher twisted his head around so far that his nose was over the nape of his neck, but it was only the garter that he abused this way; outside, in front of the door, the student was unscathed. But from that moment he never again dared to wear a garter on his right leg.

The three students were now well rid of their teacher. However, the rich man's two sons, who had been living on credit for so long, could not leave the city before they settled their debts. They were incarcerated until they could pay everything they owed. The poor man's son was now wealthier than them because he had no debts, and he was left free to do what he liked. However, he refused to abandon his friends, and went to see them in prison to discuss their situation. He thought they could write to their father to ask him to extricate them from their predicament. "We will not do anything," they told him. "We are fully aware that it would be of no use, because he is so irritated that we disobeyed him that he won't send us the smallest penny. But you are so intelligent that you could get some money. You are the man to deceive the devil in person, if necessary." He had little desire to do this, but he felt obliged to try to rescue them because they had always treated him well, so he promised that he would see what he could do.

We know full well that his studies at the black school had not been a waste of time, because he changed a garter into man and he knew how to summon the old Eric.* That very evening he went to the cemetery. Three times he walked around the church backwards, and each time he passed the front door he whistled through the keyhole while reciting magic spells. When he finished his third time around the church, the old Eric appeared, none other than the little gray master with a lame foot with whom they had studied earlier. "What do you want?" the summoned one asked friendlily, thinking it was preferable to use kindness with his former student in order to get him under his power. "I need money," replied the student, "and I ask you to loan me a bushel."

"Fine, you shall have one that is full to the brim, and I will be happy to get one scraped to the bottom back at the end of three years, but if you don't reimburse me, you will belong to me body and soul." He was convinced that the lad's two comrades would quickly run through the money, and that there was no way they would be able to return the whole amount to him, nor even half of the loan, at the end of three years. "Those are very modest conditions," replied the student. "I ask permission from you to settle the debt before the time is up, if that's possible." The old Eric accepted this without haggling, and a minute later returned with a bushel full of sparkling silver coins. The student took out a scarf that he placed beneath the bushel, took his staff, overturned the bushel and scoured it† so everything fell out on the scarf, then said to the devil: "Thanks for the loan! Here's your bushel short (of its contents), so we are quits." Being unable to object, the old Eric took back his bushel and left the money to the student. Beside himself in rage, the devil took off, leaving a terrible smell of sulfur behind. After their debts were settled, the two brothers were freed, and their comrade decided that they would leave the city to travel and see the world. The two brothers found this acceptable, but fell

---

*Gamle Erik, name of the devil in Denmark.
†There is a play on words in the text here on *Top-Skjæppe* ("Full to the brim bushel") and *strøgen skjæppe* ("bushel that has been scraped clean to the bottom").

back into their extravagant ways. Because there was no shortage of money, they squandered it until the last penny. They then promised to travel the world with their friend if he gave them travel money. "We know you can do it," they told him.

"It's a dangerous undertaking," he told them, "and this time I don't want to bear the responsibility by myself. You have to swear to follow my lead no matter what happens, and if I procure you money, you must obey me in everything." They shook hands and gave him their solemn promise. That very evening, he took them to a cemetery and summoned the old Eric again. "You again!" the devil exclaimed. "I thank you much for what you did the last time! You got one over on me, but it could be said you can't do without me. What do you want now?"

"My comrades and I want to travel, but we need money. Would you be kind enough to give us some?"

"I am very good-natured," old Eric replied, "but my motto is give and take. Since we are old acquaintances, I'm going to help you without asking to be paid back. I will give you an inexhaustible purse that you can keep for three years while you visit the world, but in return, I request this of you: starting tomorrow, and until the end of the three years, you can only say a single phrase. One of you will say 'we three,' the second will say 'for the money,' and the third, 'that's right.' If one of you says anything else, then all three of you will belong to me." They accepted and returned to the inn.

During that night, they agreed on the following: the poor man's son would keep the purse and pay all expenses. And they loudly promised that none of them would speak any other words than those that had been imposed on them. Whatever might happen to them, they were all convinced that it could not be worse than falling into the devil's hands. They traveled from one land to the next, seeing all the world's wonders and always managing to get by speaking the three phrases. Of course everyone everywhere took them for simpletons, but because they paid well, the innkeepers were satisfied. Three days before the three years were up, they came to a strange city and went into a good inn. They were well dressed and outfitted, and the innkeeper came out to welcome them and ask what they wanted. "We three," said the first.

"These three gentlemen wish to lodge together," said the man. "That is totally possible."

"For money," said the second.

"Obviously," replied the innkeeper, "we must make a living."

"That's right," said the third. Their host fully agreed, and had not yet seen anything abnormal in their behavior. They were not very chatty and perhaps not very clever, but this was often the case with distinguished people; he was used to it. Our three companions went into the dining room, still mute. After a minute, the innkeeper came to take their order. "We three," said the first.

"For money," said the second.

"That's right," said the third.

The innkeeper found this a bit peculiar, but he set the table where they were going to dine. He asked them if they wanted to drink and got the same answers, and when a stranger who was present tried to join the conversation, wanting to know if they had already visited this city, and got the same answers, he shut his mouth, and the innkeeper was convinced they were simpletons.

At this same time, another traveler had come to stay at the inn, and the innkeeper noticed that he was carrying a large sum of money. He told his wife this would be a golden opportunity to become rich without having anything to worry about—they could murder the rich traveler and accuse the three simpletons of the crime. His wife, being no better than him, had often helped him rob his guests, and was ready to take part in this infamy. In the middle of the night, when everyone in the inn was sound asleep, the couple slipped into the traveler's room, slit his throat, took all his money, and left the bloody knife in a bag belonging to one of the three simpletons.

Early the next day, the innkeeper quickly set off to fetch the authorities to tell them that a traveler had been killed in his bed at his inn. "I am in total despair, I have no idea who is guilty," he said. These servants of the court made their way to the inn. They thoroughly searched it and eventually found the knife. The three companions were made to get up, and were immediately interrogated. The judge asked them: "Which of you killed the traveler?"

"We three," answered the first.

"I really doubt that all three of you had a hand in the murder," the judge replied. "But why did you do it?"

"For money," said the second.

"I fully understand why you did it: to steal his money."

"That's right," added the third.

"God preserve us from a right like that!* You shall pay for your crime!" Because they confessed and all evidence pointed to them, the verdict was delivered instantly. The three of them would be hanged on the following day; there was no need to wait. The three years during which they could only say the three phrases were up that same next day, but they stuck to it, preferring death on the gallows to falling into the clutches of the devil, therefore thwarting his dark design. Of course he had inspired the innkeeper to murder his guest, thinking by this he would capture the students, but they accepted their death sentence even though they were innocent, so his efforts would not be rewarded.

The next day, the three unfortunate lads were brought on a cart to the execution site. A crowd was hurrying there because the homicide had stirred a lot of emotion. A priest stood there to urge them to repent before suffering their punishment, but even he was

---

*A play on words of the two meanings of the Danish *ret,* "justice/law" and "right," like the word *Recht* in German.

not able to draw any confessions from them except the words, "We three, for money, that's right."

"May God help us if that's true," he cried, and continued encouraging them to repent. The innkeeper, who was standing in the middle of the crowd, yelled: "Let's finish this, let justice be done!" The priest spoke a few more words, then stopped, and the three condemned men were led to the gallows and the rope was placed around their necks.

At that very moment a carriage drawn by four horses arrived, and a white handkerchief was shaken out a window. The executioners stopped what they were doing, thinking it might be a messenger from the king granting clemency. The carriage came to a stop right next to the gallows. A man dressed in black got out and handed the students a piece of paper—their contract. "Now you may speak freely," he told them, before turning to the judge and saying: "Seize the innkeeper. His wife and he committed the murder. They hid the money in their cellar, where they also stashed the blood-covered clothing." The stranger got back into his carriage and left, without anyone knowing where. The innkeeper was immediately arrested. The stolen objects as well as the blood-stained garments were found, and he and his wife both confessed their crime. They were condemned and hanged the next day.

The three students were now free as the air, but the purse had disappeared because its time was up, and they didn't have a penny between them. They sold their luggage for a little money and headed back out on the road. The Evil One's carriage passed them and he stuck his head out the window to yell, "I got two of them!"—namely the innkeeper and his wife, with whom he had to be satisfied for the time being.

The students pursued their path. They had studied and traveled, they had risked body and soul, and now they pined for home. But this was not easily taken care of, for they were a long ways from home and were no longer able, as they had once intended, to take the money needed for the journey from the purse before it vanished. Their incarceration had prevented this. Their few coins were quickly spent and they were forced to beg, but the little they got barely kept them alive. The sons of the rich man could not bear this kind of life much longer. They became ill and incapable of putting one foot in front of the other. It was not in the poor man's son's heart to let his two companions die of hunger in a foreign land, although he didn't have the least desire to try his luck with the devil again. However, he didn't see any other possibilities.

One day he summoned the devil and asked him under what conditions he would advance him a little money.* "You have gotten the better of me so often," the devil replied, "that now I no longer want any dealings with you." In reality, the devil was eager to renew ties with the student, thinking that he would eventually snare him. So he went on to say: "That doesn't matter, I am going to help you one more time. You will have the purse for a period of seven years, and you will be able to talk to your heart's content, but during this time you will not be able to put on a clean shirt, nor wash yourself, nor comb or cut your hair, nor shave, nor cut your beard and nails. If you don't make it to the end, you will belong to me after you die; however, you can keep the purse for the rest of your life. Do you consent? Otherwise I will not even give you a penny." Accepting was difficult, but the student felt it was his duty to help his friends. He therefore signed the pact and accepted the purse.

He took care of his two companions until they had recovered their strength, then gave them money to travel—just enough to get home. He then bid them farewell. "I cannot accompany you," he explained, "because I swore an oath that I want to accomplish." He told them nothing more. Deeply distressed by having to separate,

---

*The Danish word used here is *penge,* which corresponds to the English penny and the German *pfennig.*

they thanked him wholeheartedly for everything he had done for them. They then returned home, and we hear no more of them.

The young man was now alone, and had to spend the next seven years respecting the harsh conditions that had been imposed on him. He therefore went to an inn whose owner he trusted greatly, for he had stayed there before. "I've sworn an oath to shut myself away from everything for a long time," he told him, "and to have no relations with people at all." He rented a room for a good price and lived there, year after year, under the severe constraints the devil had imposed on him, thinking that over time the student would eventually give up trying to fulfill them. The student ordered all the books he could and read so much that he had soon absorbed all the erudition of the world. Every week he would give his host a large sum of money to distribute among the poor, something that drove the devil wild with rage. When six years had passed without the student breaking one of the prohibitions, the Evil One began to sweat with anxiety, fearing that the student would once more find a way to get out of his snare.

The young man looked horrible. He resembled an animal more than a man, covered in filth, with long hair and claws on his hands and feet. He refused to show himself to anyone and had his meals brought into one room while he waited in another. He had arranged his windows so that no one could see inside but he could still see out of them. To pass the time, he often watched people coming and going, rich and poor going about their business while he had buried himself alive. After he had lived here for six years, a vehicle that often passed by his windows caught his attention. It was not so much the vehicle itself that interested him as the people inside: a distinguished woman and her three daughters. All were young and beautiful but his eyes were most drawn to the youngest. Not only was she extremely beautiful, but she seemed to be charity and piety incarnate. His host told him that they were the wife and daughters of a local landowner, and the poor recluse could not help from spying out his window, hoping to capture even a fleeting reflection of the beautiful maiden.

The father of the three young ladies was believed to be wealthy, and he had indeed been so once, but he had succumbed to the temptations of gambling and thereby gradually lost his fortune. The day came when his debts amounted to more than the value of his farm and his other belongings. No one wished to lend him the smallest penny anymore, and he would soon be forced to go out begging, staff in hand, if he wasn't able to find help quickly. Just as he reached his wit's end, he suddenly recalled that there was an eccentric individual living at an inn whose owner he knew well, an individual no one ever saw except for this same innkeeper. He was very rich and gave out large sums to the poor. He visited the innkeeper and asked him if he might visit this strange person. "I don't think so," the innkeeper replied, "but I will ask him." When the student realized that it was the father of the three maidens who wanted to speak with him, he had him brought up. When he caught sight of this scarecrow, the farmer's first impulse was to retreat, but the young man begged him to not be afraid. "I am a man like you, not an animal or demon." The other took heart and presented his request: "Could I borrow some money from you, a large sum: three tons of gold?

"I can easily provide you this money," the student calmly replied, "if you give me one of your daughters to be my wife."

"Understood, if one will accept marrying you. I will do whatever I possibly can."

"I don't want her to accept under constraint, and want her to know what her suitor looks like." The student summoned a painter, who did a faithful portrait that the father took away with him.

He went to his eldest daughter and explained to her what was happening: "I no longer have a penny to my name and will have to leave if one of you doesn't promise to marry the man whose portrait I'm going to show you." When she saw his nails like vulture claws, she spit on the portrait and replied: "No thank you! Rather than marry a suitor like that, I would prefer our dog trainer." The man went to find his second daughter and asked her the same question. "I would rather go begging from house to house than marry a monster like that!" He then presented his request to his youngest daughter, who shuddered at the sight of the portrait. But she wanted to spare her parents and sisters from poverty, and said she would marry him. She sent him an engagement ring as proof of their troth.

When the student received the ring, he kept shaking his purse until it had spilled out the three tons of gold the farmer needed. He even shook it a few more times so that gifts could be purchased for his fiancée: golden rings and necklaces with precious stones. She barely glanced at them and locked them in a coffer that she never opened.

In the meantime, the student had a cabinetmaker craft a dozen large studded chests, each with three padlocks. "I will need them for my books," he explained, "when I leave." Every day he spent several hours shaking the purse over the chests until they were all filled with money. When he had finished his preparations, the seven years were up, and without wasting a minute he jumped into the bathtub, had his hair and nails cut, shaved off his beard, and put on some new clothes that he had had made beforehand. A beautiful vehicle drawn by four horses, which someone had purchased on his behalf, stopped in front of the door, along with three carts for his books and his chests, and he left to go to his future father-in-law's house. Of course no one recognized him, but all thought he was a very handsome young man. The two older daughters were convinced he had come as a suitor for one of them, but he addressed the farmer to ask for his youngest daughter's hand. "She is engaged," her father replied, "but I have two other daughters."

"I would like to see this youngest daughter, though," the

stranger said. Her father raised no objection, and he was escorted into a room where all three sisters were waiting. They all arose and extended their hands. He then slipped the ring that she had sent him on the youngest sister's finger and said: "This ring was given to me, and I wonder if she gives it back to me, if it will be with a good heart." She realized that he was her fiancé and gave him back the ring, this time with joy. The handsome young man moved into the farm and delighted his fiancée and the household more and more with every passing day. A month later they celebrated a splendid wedding in unconstrained joy. The two sisters felt as if they would die of jealousy when they thought how they had scorned him, and each chose to end her days prematurely. While everyone was dancing in the large ballroom, one of them went into the garden to hang herself, while the other went out to the pond and drowned herself. When the husband went out on the upper balcony, the devil stuck his head above the railing and said: "Yes, you got one, but I got two!"

The young couple lived happily together for a long time, giving joy and bliss to all those they met.

Svend Grundtvig, *Danske folkeæventyr,*
fundne i folkemunde og gjenfortalte
(Copenhagen: Reitzels Forlag, 1878), 213–235.

ATU 360.

This is a folktale that has been given a thorough literary treatment. This is easily seen by comparing it to other folktales of the same type. In Svartiskóli, *a text collected by Jón Árnason,[5] Sæmundur Sigfússon the Scholar (1056–1133) was alleged to have pursued his studies in Paris at the black school, a name bestowed on the Sorbonne! Other accounts place this diabolical school in Toledo. The school can also be found in Germanic regions, as well as France.*

10. The Soldier and the Devils

Lithuania

One day, a soldier who had fulfilled his military obligations and was returning home entered an inn. There he found a drunkard who was out of money and begged the soldier to buy him some brandy. "I don't have much," the soldier replied, "my savings is three pennies."

"Very well, buy three pennies' worth of brandy," the drunkard said, which the soldier went ahead and did.

To thank him, the drunkard offered him a cane and a knapsack. If a person touched the knapsack with the cane, it would be filled with whatever he wanted. The soldier resumed his journey, and as he crossed though a town he had an urge to smoke a pipe. He brushed the knapsack with his cane and it was immediately filled with tobacco. Later he wanted to eat. He touched the knapsack with the cane and it was instantly filled with bread.

Soon night fell. He came to a farm belonging to a well-to-do man and decided he would like to spend the night there. He asked the cook, who was busy: "Might your master give me hospitality?"

"We don't sleep here at night," the chief cook responded, "we spend it elsewhere. But go ask the master yourself."

To the soldier's question, the farm's owner replied: "You can spend the night here if you wish, and if you are not torn to pieces while you are sleeping, you'll like the lodging." The man then ordered his coachman to harness the horses to his vehicle and bring it in front of the house. Next, he and all the servants got in and left. The soldier stayed behind at the farm and went to sleep in one of the rooms. During the night, an entire band of devils entered the room and began to dance. One of the demons yelled: "I smell human flesh!" He found the soldier and overturned his bed, but the latter set it right and lay back down on it. A second did the same, but when a third one tried to imitate them, the soldier took his staff and brushed his knapsack, saying: "All the devils in the knapsack!" They all went in,[6] and the soldier spent the rest of the night quietly. In the morning, his host came back and asked him: "Very well, what have you seen?" He told him, then asked: "Do you have many threshers in the barn?"

"I have six." The soldier brought the devils there and ordered the servants with the threshers* to strike the knapsack with all their might. They got down to work and all the devils began screeching. When the soldier thought they had gotten their fill, he carried the knapsack to a pond near the farm and emptied it in the water. He then returned to the farm. His host asked him: "Are these devilish hauntings going to now stop in my house?"

"Certainly," the soldier replied.

"As thanks, I am giving you my daughter's hand and half of my fields!" he said, and the wedding was soon celebrated. One day the soldier was inspecting the fields with his wife, and they came to the pond into which he had thrown the devils. He felt an urge to bathe, so he took off his shirt and dove in, but one of the devils who had survived grabbed him, shouting: "I've got you, assassin! You are going to die."

"Let me say farewell to my wife," the soldier replied. The demon allowed him to get out of the water. He went back to his wife, whom he grabbed and lifted off her feet. The devil waited and waited for the soldier to come back, but in vain. In the end, he went to the bank, and saw that the soldier had another kind of bag (it was his wife), and said: "Ah, you still want to beat me to death! That's fine, I spare you," and he scampered off as fast as he could.

August Leskien & K. Brugman, *Litauische Volkslieder und Märchen* (Strasbourg: Trübner, 1882), 410–412.

ATU 330 B, BP 2, 157–163, Mlex 103–1036, EM 12, 111–120.

---

*Those who beat the wheat on the estate.

11. Cathy and the Devil

Bohemia

Once in a village there lived a peasant named Cathy. She owned a small house and garden and had some small savings. But even if she were living in the lap of luxury, she would not have found a husband, even the poorest one, because she was as mean as the devil and a malicious gossip. She lived with her old mother and sometimes needed help. But no one would come help her, even if she offered to pay them in ducats. She would quibble over the smallest trifle and yelled so loud that she could be heard for ten leagues in every direction. To top it off, she was dreadful, and at the age of forty had never had a suitor.

As is customary in many villages, people played music every Sunday afternoon. When the bagpipe was heard at the tavern, the room filled quickly with young men while the women stood in front of the building, Cathy in front, and the children at the windows. The men would wave to the women, who would then join them inside the tavern. Cathy never had this opportunity, although she might have been able to bribe the bagpipe player. But despite this, she could never miss a Sunday. One day, as she was going to the tavern again, she said to herself: "At my age, I've never danced with a man—it's irritating! By my faith, I would dance today even with the devil."

In a rage, she entered the tavern and watched the single men inviting the unmarried women. A man dressed as a hunter came in. He sat down near her and asked for something to drink. The innkeeper brought him a pitcher of beer. The man took it and offered Cathy a drink. She was a bit surprised by the honor he showed her and turned him down initially, but eventually agreed, with goodwill. The man set down the pitcher and took out a ducat that he tossed to the bagpipe player, asking him to play a solo. The men drew away from the center of the room, and the man invited Cathy to dance.

"Good heavens, who could that be?" the old people whispered. The young men grimaced, and the young women hid behind one another and hid their faces behind their aprons so that Cathy would not see that they were mocking her. But she saw nothing, so happy was she to be dancing, and even if the entire world were making sport of her she would not have cared. The gentleman danced all afternoon and evening with Cathy, bought her spice bread and Rosoglio,* and when the time to return home arrived, he accompanied her all through the village. "If only I could dance with you like today until the day I die!" Cathy said when it came time to say goodbye.

"Why not? Come with me."

"Where do you live?"

"Hang on to my neck and I will tell you."

He stopped at the entrance to his home, knocked, and his acolytes opened the door. Seeing him dripping with sweat, they wanted to lay Cathy on the ground to give him some relief. But she clung so tightly to the devil that it was impossible to dislodge her. For better or worse, he had to go seek out Lucifer with Cathy clinging to his neck. "Who are you bringing here?" Lucifer asked.

"I went to Earth," the devil answered. "I heard Cathy complaining about finding no one to dance with her, so to console her, I danced with her, and then planned to give her a tour of hell. I never imagined," he concluded, "that she wouldn't want to let me go."

"If only you would listen to what I tell you, you three times a fool!" the older Lucifer barked at him in reply. "Before establishing a relationship with anyone, you have to know his or her state of mind. If you had thought of that before accompanying her here,

---

*Brandy that has sugar and rose essence added to it.

you would never have brought her. Now, be off like the wind and get rid of her!"

Extremely annoyed, the devil returned with the lady Catherine. He promised her the earth if she let him go, then he cursed her, but nothing worked. Worn out and furious, he came to a field, still bearing his burden. There a young shepherd, wearing a gigantic hide, was watching over his sheep. The devil transformed into an ordinary man, and the shepherd failed to recognize him. "What are you carrying there, buddy?" he asked amicably.

"Ah, my friend, I am completely out of breath. Here's how it is: I'm peacefully traveling along, thinking of nothing, this woman hanging on my neck, and I would be happy to drop her for anything in the world. I planned to carry her to the next village to free myself, but I am no longer capable of doing it—my legs are too wobbly."

"I'm going to help you out, but not for too long, as I have to take my animals to pasture. I will carry her about half the way."

"This makes me happy!" Then addressing Cathy, the shepherd said: "Hang on to my neck!"

Immediately letting go of the devil, she gripped the shepherd by the gigantic hide that he had only just that morning borrowed from the steward. He, too, soon had his fill and began contemplating ways he could get rid of Cathy. On reaching a pond, he asked himself if he might not be able to throw her in it, but how? Would it be possible to remove the hide to which she was clinging? Because this hide was quite large, he slipped it off little by little. First he got his hand out and she didn't notice. He then got his second hand out and began undoing the buttons. He undid the first, then the second. Finally he undid the third and—plop!—Cathy and the hide were dropped into the pond.

The devil hadn't followed the shepherd, as he had stayed behind to keep watch over the sheep. He sat down on the ground to await their master's return. He did not have long to wait; the shepherd, with the water-soaked hide over his shoulders, was running back to his flock, fearing that the stranger may have already headed to the village, leaving the sheep to fend for themselves. When they caught sight of each other, they both stopped and stared: the devil saw that the shepherd was returning without Cathy, and the shepherd saw that the gentleman was still there. Once they shepherd had described what had happened, the devil exclaimed: "My greatest thanks! You have done me a huge favor, otherwise I would have had to drag Catherine with me until the Final Judgment. I will never forget what you have done for me, and will greatly reward you for it one day. But just so you know who you've pulled out of an embarrassing fix, know that I am the devil," and he vanished. The shepherd stood stupefied for a good minute, then told himself: "If they are all as stupid as that one, then things are just fine."

A young prince was the ruler of the land in which the shepherd lived. He was immensely rich and, because he was master of all, he did whatever he wanted whenever he wanted. He spent his days amusing himself in every possible way, and once night fell, all could hear the unbridled singing of his drinking companions. His two high officials, who were no better, governed the country. Whatever the prince didn't squander they kept for themselves, and their poor subjects lived in poverty. One day, when the prince was at a loss for something new to do, he summoned his astrologer and commanded him to predict his future, as well as that of the two governors. The astrologer obediently complied with the prince's wishes and read the stars to learn the fate of the three men. "Forgive me, O Prince," he said when he finished, "but such danger threatens all three of you I hardly dare reveal it to you."

"Whatever it is, say it! But you will have to remain here, and if your prediction doesn't come true, it will cost you your head."

"I will obey your command. Listen! Before the full moon, the devil will come to fetch your two governors, and when the moon is full, he will come back for you, O Prince, and carry you all off alive to hell."

"Throw this wretched liar into the dungeon!" the prince ordered, and his servants carried out this command.

But deep down, the prince was not as valiant as he claimed. The astrologer's words had left their mark on him. For the first time in his life, he felt the stirrings of conscience. His two governors, half dead from fear, were taken back to their palace rooms. Neither of them could eat a thing. Eventually, they gathered together everything they owned, saddled their horses, and went back to their castles and had them barricaded on all sides to make it impossible for the devil to get in. The prince began following the straight and narrow path, living an austere and quiet life taking care of his kingdom, in hopes of changing his fate.

The shepherd knew nothing of all this, and continued taking his sheep out to graze without any care about events in the world outside. One day, the devil loomed up in front of him and said, "Shepherd, I have come to do you the favor that I owe you. I have to carry off your prince's former governors, for they have given bad advice and robbed the poor. When the day comes, go to the first castle, where a large crowd will have gathered together. Once you hear screams coming from the dwelling, have the governor's lackeys open the gate to you, and as I am carrying off their master, approach me and say: 'Vanish, or he will cook you!' I will obey you and go away, but demand two bags of gold from the chatelaine. If he refuses, threaten to summon me back. Then go to the second castle, do the same thing, and demand the same payment. Use this money to do good. When the moon is full, I will come back to fetch the prince in person, but I advise you against trying to free him, for it will cost you your life."

The shepherd took note of every word. When the moon reached its first quarter, he left his job and made his way to the first governor's castle. He arrived at the designated spot. A crowd was pushing toward it, waiting for the devil to bring the governor out. A desperate scream rose out of the castle, the gates opened, and out came the devil, dragging the nobleman, who was as white as a sheet and seemed already half dead. The shepherd approached, grabbed the devil by the hand while shouting: "Vanish, or he will cook you!" The demon fled at once, and delirious with joy the governor kissed the shepherd's two hands, asking him what he wanted as a reward. "Two bags of gold!" he replied, and the governor ordered that they be given to him at once.

Quite satisfied, the shepherd made his way to the second castle, where everything turned out just as well. It's easy to see that the prince would soon hear about him, as he was always asking his governors for news. Once warned, he sent a carriage for the shepherd, and upon his arrival at the palace, the prince instantly begged him to take pity on him and save him from the devil's clutches, too. "My lord and master," the shepherd replied, "I cannot make you any promise, as my life is at stake and you are a great sinner. But if you wish to atone, act justly, and govern with wisdom and clemency as behooves a prince, I will try, even if it means going to hell in your place." The prince swore to mend his ways and the shepherd left, promising he would be there at the designated moment.

Everyone waited for the full moon with trepidation and anxiety. Whatever the prince's subjects' feelings toward him had been before, they now looked upon him with pity because, from the moment he changed, you could not wish for a better prince. The days went by, in joy for some and in pain for others, and before the prince had even realized it, the day had come when he would have to part from everything he loved. Dressed in black, as if attending a funeral, the prince sat down to wait for the shepherd or the devil. The door suddenly flew open and the devil was standing there. He ordered the prince: "Prepare yourself, your time has come and I am here to take you!" Not saying a word, the prince rose and followed the devil into the courtyard that was swarming with people. In a sweat, the shepherd hastily carved a path through the crowd, and when he reached the devil he roared: "Run, run, otherwise something bad will happen to you!"

"How dare you hold me back? Did you forget what I whispered in your ear?"

"Idiot, it's not the prince I'm thinking of, but you! Cathy is still alive and she is looking for you."

When he heard that name, the devil vanished as if carried away by the wind, and left the prince alone. The shepherd silently laughed at him, happy he could save the prince thanks to his ruse. The monarch named him first gentleman of the court and loved him like a brother. He did the right thing in doing so, as the shepherd was a loyal counselor and faithful servant. He did not even keep a single coin from his four bags of money, but used them to compensate all the people the governors had robbed.

JOSEPH WENZIG, *WESTLAWISCHER MÄRCHENSCHATZ*
(LEIPZIG: LORCK, 1857), 165–74.

12. The Old Woman Who Outwitted the Devil

Lithuania

In a village there once lived a young farmer who had married a pretty woman. They loved each other so much they never fought; they always spoke lovingly to each other and kissed constantly. One day the devil, who was traveling, came and paid them a visit. He was greatly surprised at how well they got along, and wanted to disrupt their relationship. But no matter what he did, nothing came of it. After many attempts, drunk with rage, he resumed his journey, while spilling his bile.

He was walking along when he met an old beggar woman who asked him: "Hail friend, why are you frothing like that?'

"Why would I tell you?" retorted the devil in fury. "In any event, you would not be able to help me!"

"Don't you know that we old women know and understand a great many things? Just tell me your problem and I might be able to help you, as I've done so many times for others."

The devil paused in thought: "Hold on, the old woman may be very cunning." He told her why he was so angry. "Just imagine, I spent six months in the village of this young married couple. They get along so well that I could never sow any discord between them. I failed, so who would not be furious about wasting so much time for nothing?"

"That's child's play for me," the old woman replied. "I'm going to restore your honor to you." The devil was elated, and asked her what she wanted in exchange. "A pair of rope shoes and a pair of Strasbourg-style leather shoes," she told him. The Prince of Evil promised her he would give her the very best ones to be had. Once they had concluded their agreement, the old woman advised the devil to not stray too far, for she intended to take action that very day.

They reached the village, where they found the young wife alone at home while her husband was working in the fields. The old woman went in and asked for alms. After receiving some, she began to chat about this and that to get in her good graces. "My dear little heart, you are beautiful and respectable; your little husband can truly be happy that he married you. I know that you and he live in the most perfect harmony, like no other couple in the world. My little chick, I'm going to teach you how to strengthen your bonds even more so that never will an unpleasant word upset your beautiful relationship."

"Tell me, "said the young woman, "I will give you a huge reward."

"Not far from the top of your husband's head there is a gray hair that you have to shave clear off without his noticing. Once you have done that, you will experience even greater love for the rest of your life."

The young woman believed her and asked her how she could do it without her husband noticing. "When you bring him his lunch, suggest taking a little nap while he lays his head on your knees, and once he falls asleep, take out your razor and cut the gray hair." This all persuaded the young woman, who bid the old woman farewell after thanking her from the bottom of her heart and giving her all she could carry.

The old woman then visited the husband who was working his fields. "Hello, honey!"

"Thank you, my dear old woman!" Once they had greeted each other, the old woman asked him to take a break. The oxen could also benefit from taking a rest. He stopped working and asked her: "What do you want?"

"Very well, my dear boy, my little darling, I hardly dare tell you as it has caused me such fright," and she began to sob horribly.

"But what's the matter, tell me!" Still sobbing the old woman replied: "I know that you and your little wife get along wonderfully well, but God keep you! She plans to murder you so she can marry someone else who is richer than you. I was with her just a short while ago, when I learned of this horrific thing." These words terrified the boy, who asked her if she knew when and how his wife planned to do it. "This afternoon, when she brings you your lunch," she answered, "she will have a razor in her pocket. She will invite you to rest your head in her lap so that you can take a little nap after your meal, and once you are sleeping, she will cut your throat." He thanked her feverishly for this information, and promised to reward her later. The old woman then hid in a field of wheat to watch how the couple would fall out.

When noon approached, the woman took her husband's razor and put it in her pocket. In great agitation, the man waited for noon to learn if the old woman had told him the truth. When his wife was there, they embraced and kissed as they always did, and he sat down to eat lunch. Once he had finished, she said: "You must be tired, come take a little nap, place your head on my knees." He complied, and after a minute pretended that he had fallen asleep, so he could see if the old woman had been lying or not.

When she thought he was sound asleep, his wife gently removed the razor from her pocket to cut off the gray hair, but he saw her, jumped up fast as lightning, grabbed her head, tore off her scarf, then, holding her hair, punched her repeatedly. "Monster, murderer, wild beast, animal, you showed me kindness and pretended you loved me, all the better to kill me! I'm going to give you a lesson that will stop you from ever thinking of doing such a foul deed ever again." She begged him to stop, but it was no use; he beat her brutally until he fell down in exhaustion.

The devil was sitting on a stone nearby and keeping watch. When he saw what happened he clapped and laughed himself sick. But soon even he began to feel horrified and disgusted at the old woman's infamous perfidy. He thought, "She is more evil than me. People say the devil is always responsible whenever anything goes wrong, but just look what women like this are capable of!" He handed her the promised shoes at the end of a long stick, telling her: "I don't want to go anywhere near you, because you seem quite capable of bewitching me into getting a good beating, too. You are worse and even more twisted than I am." Once she took the shoes, he threw the stick as far as he could and was off like a shot. For her part, the old woman set off on her way again, happy to see she was wilier than the devil and able to frighten him so much that he fled.

AUGUST SCHLEICHER, *LITAUISCHE MÄRCHEN, SPIRCHWORTE, RÄTSEL UND LIEDER* (WEIMAR: BÖHLAU, 1857), ATU 1353, 350–53.

13. The Devil Is Beaten

Switzerland

A peasant, buried in debt, whose last cow had just kicked the bucket, left his barn in despair. He crossed through the village and raced onto the open road. It was Saint Martin's Eve and the rent was due, but he had spent his last penny buying bread! Lost in his dark thoughts, he began dawdling on the road; the blue sky and the rocky cliffs felt reassuring. He had the impression that there was something in the air, as if a miracle had occurred, something great and rare as sometimes happens, when some unexpected stroke of good fortune will fall in the lap of some poor bugger.

Immediately after the last house, at a fork in the road, a man like no one he had ever seen before gave him a friendly greeting and asked where he was going. The peasant felt like something was trying to pull him back into the village. With a final burst of energy he braced himself against this invisible force and shared his distress with the stranger: "My cellar and attic are empty, and if I can't pay my rent, I'll be out in the street."

"This is good timing," the stranger said in a strongly nasal voice. "You are in need of money and I need a soul that I acquired honestly! If you give me a task that I accomplish in one day then your soul will belong to me. If I can't do it, this purse is yours. Take it and put it on your belt. Throw away your rags and comport yourself like a master. Who has money has power; he gives the orders and the poor obey them." His spiel overcame any objections the fellow might have had. Captivated by the devilish gaze and the clinking of coins, he really did not give much thought to his objections, although he had guessed the stranger was the devil because of his forked hooves and mephitic breath. "Give me your purse. I am going to suggest a task for you to do, and if you finish it in one day, I will be your lackey."

First thing in the morning, they left the village and went into the immense wilderness that, since the river had disappeared, had grown wild. As far as the eye could see there were ponds, groves of birch and alder, barberry bushes, and vines. Nobody would be capable of clearing and working this wilderness in a year, not to mention a single day! "Plough this terrain for me," he demanded, showing it to the Prince of Evil. Around noon he came back to see how the work was advancing. Horrified, with his heart in his throat and his eyes starting from their sockets, he stared at the beautiful arable land still smoking. What had become of the groves of birch and alder, the dark pools, the tangled expanses of blackberry bushes and brambles? Furrows were neatly plowed side by side, and flocks of crows were pecking and scratching the soil, having a feast. A small parcel still remained in a wild state in the distance, at the very edge of this former wilderness, a small plot of land that the Horned One finished in no time at all. Stricken, the peasant trudged back to the village, wiping the sweat from his brow. "What happened to you?" asked a small old woman he had never seen before. "Did you swallow some thorns?"

"It would have been better if it were me that swallowed them instead of the other," he replied irately.

But because he presumed that the small woman might be able to pull him out of his predicament, he told her of his problem without any further ado. "Go home and have a quiet lunch. If the devil has finished preparing the field, he is going to want to take a break. You will then order him to turn black wool white, to dip his claws in a holy water stoup, then to tear out one of your hairs and hold it straight as a candle. These are three tasks; one alone will be enough to give him a hard time. You will see how he clears his throat and squirms because of how uncomfortable this makes him. Follow my advice and you will not regret it!" After having snorted, the old woman left, dragging in her old wooden shoes. "That woman is not trustworthy," he thought. "Perhaps she is of diabolical origin, too." He shivered, although the bees were buzzing, the heat was shimmering off the groves, and the water of the streams was flowing in trickles.

When the noon bell sounded, the devil entered, squinting his eyes and spitting out green sparks. "The land has been plowed," he drawled nasally. "Go over there to verify the quality of my work."

"Give yourself an hour to rest," the peasant urged him, "it's the custom with us here."

He leaned over his shoes to hide his anxiety, and once the devil had gone away, he opened the window to take a breath before leaving to go inspect the fields. Wringing his hands in despair and raising his arms toward heaven, he begged: "Can't I get some decent advice, something enlightening that would allow me to impose a task on this cunning enemy, a task that will keep him busy with no let-up until evening?"

At that moment he ran into his cousin. "You showed up in the nick of time," he said to her, pulling himself together. "Put down your load and help me. Here is a gold piece." He indirectly described to her the kind of fix in which he found himself. "If I don't find a task for the devil, I am lost." His cousin spit on the gold coin, threw it down in the street, and took off at once.

As if he had been hit in the head, the peasant staggered back home, threw himself down on a bench, and thought: "I have no black wool and the holy water stoup is empty; all I can do is try the hair." Weary and resigned, he stood up when he heard a knock on the door. He consigned himself to God and decided to try the hair no matter what happened. "Here is something to keep you busy," he told the devil. "Hold this hair up so that it is as straight as the letter "I" without breaking it, and if you succeed, I am yours."

With an easy smile, Satan prepared himself and took the hair between his thumb and index finger, as if he wanted to thread a needle. He spit in his hands, smoothed it out, and caressed it while he grumbled and grimaced. The more effort he put into winning this wager, the more the recalcitrant hair twisted and curved around itself, until it eventually broke.

Facing him, the peasant enjoyed the futile attempts of the Prince of Evil more and more. First he smiled, then he clicked his tongue, and finally he doubled over laughing. The beaten devil cursed and raged: "Bury this hair in the throat of the witch who gave you this advice!" He fled the scene, leaving behind such a pestilential odor that the peasant thought it might kill him.

JOHANNES JERGERLEHNER, WALLITZER SAGEN
(LEIPZIG: H. HAESSEL VERLAG, 1922), 89–91.

14. The Smith of Rumpelbach

Austrian Tyrol

The smith of Rumpelbach had always been a very brave and active man. However he also had the misfortune of having money owed to him by individuals who were reluctant to loosen their purse strings even when their purses were bulging with money. As he had never had much food in which to sink his teeth despite all his hard work, he became gloomier by the day, and one night asked himself if there might not be some medicinal herb nearby underground capable of curing his debtors' greed. However he did not know how to find the doctor that might bring him some. As we all know, the devil is a lord who does not need to be prayed to for long. The next day the smith went to his forge where he grabbed his hammer, feeling both anxious and glum. But look! An elegant small lord wearing a green tailcoat, with a dagger at his side and a rifle on his back, showed up at the door. "How are you doing, blacksmith of Rumpelbach?" he asked cordially.

"Oh, not terrible. I have plenty of work but not plenty of money."

"Slaving away without earning money is like sowing without harvesting!" Little inclined to chat, the smith harshly yelled at the nob: "It's not your fine words that will help me!"

"You imagine that I would be incapable of helping you?" scoffed the other, slightly lifting his hat in order to allow the smith to get a glimpse of a small twisted horn.

"Oh, so it's really you," replied the other, politely removing his filthy cap. "We should be able to do business together."

"Why not? You should know, though, that for all services rendered I will demand nothing less than your soul, and I will come to fetch it in seven years at the very latest."

These words froze the blood of our hero. He remained mute for a moment, seeking a loophole, without having the courage to contradict the devil. The latter looked at the poltroon sarcastically and pretended he was leaving, but the other held him back: "Let's try it! Here is what I want in exchange for my soul: a bench in front of my house. Whoever sits on it will not be able to get off without my consent."

"Easy!" the devil quickly burst in to say. "Go ahead, sign."

"Slow down, you!" the smith replied. "It's not that simple. My soul is worth more than a simple bench. I also need a cherry tree—whoever climbs it cannot get down unless I say they can. And as you can never take two without a third, also give me a sack. Whoever goes in will not be able to get out without my permission; then my soul will be yours."

The devil joyfully accepted and pulled from his pocket a large ledger in which the contract was recorded, which the smith had to sign in his own blood. The devil left and soon came back with the bag, the bench, and the tree. It might seem surprising that he could carry all that, but is there anything that the devil can't do? The sack went into the depths of the forge, the bench in front of the house, and the tree in the garden. The devil sincerely pitched in and when the work was finished, he shouted, "In seven years!" and took off.

Barely had the devil vanished from sight when a corpulent peasant woman, whose husband often carried off ironwork from the forge without ever pulling out his wallet, passed by. "Welcome!" the smith called out. "What are you in such a hurry for! What's the latest news in the village? Come sit on the bench next to me and tell me everything." The woman, unaware of the bone of contention between her man and the smith, sat down on the bench because gossiping was her business. She told him everything from A to Z, and while giving it another go, starting from the beginning again, she saw that the moon was already climbing over the neighboring mountain. She realized that she had been chatting for a long time and tried to stand up to go back home. What a fright she had when she vainly tried to get up and heard the smith, who was laughing uncontrollably, exclaim: "You're caught! You will never be able to escape until your husband pays me what he owes." He went inside to dine and go to bed.

The next morning around dawn, the smith heard a violent knocking at his door. He went down to see who was making this racket and found the peasant woman's husband, who offered him three times what he owed, if only he freed his Ursule. Satisfied, the smith accepted, and the other, mortified, took off with his wife.

They had barely disappeared when a young boy, whose father had not left the smith a fond memory, came racing by. "Hey kid," he said, "would you like some cherries?"

"Why wouldn't I want them? Give me some!"

"Climb the tree over there in the yard and eat your fill!"

The scamp didn't wait to be told twice. In less time than it takes to say it, he was in the cherry tree, and watching him eat was a glorious sight. But, woe! When he tried to climb down, he remained stuck there. The smith came by soon to look over his latest catch. Sobbing, the child asked to be freed from his lofty prison, but with no success. "You will not come down so long as your father hasn't paid me," the smith replied. It wasn't until about

noon that the child's father passed behind the smith's house looking for his son. When he caught sight of him in the tree, he began
yelling furiously: "Why won't you climb down from there, you
little pig?"

"I can't," whined the child, showing his father how all his
efforts to climb down were futile.

Then the smith appeared, laughing uproariously. "What a
fine catch this bird is! Now pay me quickly, otherwise your son
can stay there for eternity!" The peasant saw what was what and
quickly pulled out his purse and paid the smith three times what
he was owed. The child felt as if he had been untied, and he raced
back home as fast as he could with his humiliated father.

Feeling quite smug, the smith pocketed the money. He was
thinking about the best way to use his sack when a young woman
passed by. She was wiggling like an excited poodle because she was
soon to marry. It so happened that her fiancé was one of the dead-
beats for whom the smith had asked the devil for the bench, the
cherry tree, and the sack. Margot greeted him cordially: "Good
afternoon, master smith. How are you?"

"How can you ask me that? We do well when we have money.
But come here, Margot, and come look at the new thing in my
smithy. Have you ever seen a sack like this in all your life?"

They went in and he pulled his enormous diabolical sack from
a corner. "Golly," said the girl as she burst out laughing. "There
is enough room inside that for me to dance the waltz with my
Pierrot."

"So dance then!" the smith said mockingly. He dropped the
sack over the girl's head and pulled it down until it covered her
completely, despite her pleas and prayers.

She had to remain in this dark lodging until her fiancé came
to free her. A ball had been announced for that evening at the Inn
of the Gray Bear. Pierrot wanted to go, and had been looking for
Margot all day to no avail. In his distress, he passed by the forge,

where he could hear her crying and pleading. "Where are you? Why are you crying?" he said, quite surprised. The smith came by just then, and without beating around the bush told him, "It means you have to pay me right now, otherwise the next time you see her will be on Judgment Day!" Pierrot was surprised, although he knew full well why this was happening. When he found his Margot in the sack, he quickly paid the smith three times more than he owed him, then took off with his darling.

The smith developed a liking for these tricks, and in a very short while had amassed quite a fortune. The years flew by and the seventh was coming toward its end. Though the day was drawing nearer when the Prince of Evil would come to fetch him, the smith remained calm and untroubled. On the first day of the eighth year, the little dandy dressed in green entered the forge and politely invited the smith to follow him. "I'll be ready in just a moment," the latter replied. "I just want to finish this horseshoe. While you are waiting, you can go sit on the bench outside, for you must surely be tired." The devil didn't see anything wrong in this offer and took a seat, but he soon realized that getting off the bench was another story! He began begging the smith to free him, and the man replied: "If you grant me another seven years here, I will let you go." The devil eventually agreed, and in a state of great irritation took to his heels.

During the next seven years, the smith never missed an opportunity to turn the bench, the cherry tree, and the sack to his best advantage. But time flew, and before he knew it the first day of the eighth year was upon him. The little dandy dressed in green showed up at the forge early that morning, and could not have been any friendlier. "Very well, master, are we going to head out?"

"Give me just another fifteen minutes and I will have finished this chain. I have a beautiful cherry tree in the yard, full of delicious sweet cherries. Take advantage of them, for you are surely tired and hungry. I'll go put up the ladder."

No sooner said than done. A minute later the devil was in the tree and realized he had fallen into a trap. He had to once again promise the smith that he would come back to fetch him in seven years. He had once again been made a laughingstock, and had to return to hell alone.

During the seven years that followed, the bench, tree, and sack got quite a workout. A time soon came when no one was in debt to the smith with the devilish reputation, and all went in fear of his evil tricks. Our hero, now one of the richest in the area, was anxiously wondering if he could pull one over on the devil a third time. The long dreaded day finally arrived, and with it the Prince of Evil in his most beautiful finery. "So, Mr. Smith, the seven years are over and done! Today we shall go to my grandmother's house." Disconcerted at first, our hero quickly got a hold of himself. "My dear lord, be patient for a moment! I promised my neighbor that I would shoe his horse, and I would be the worst kind of rogue if I didn't keep my word. I'm going to go get his horse right away. To save time, would you be kind enough to get thirty-two nails out of the sack over there?" The smith left and this oafish devil got into the sack to fetch the nails that were all the way at the bottom. When the smith returned with the animal, he found the devil shouting with all his might from inside the sack: "Alas, alas, I will never get out! Free me! I will do everything you ask me to." The smith's heart almost burst with joy when he saw his ruse had worked, and he said, "If you swear to abandon all rights you hold over me, I will let you leave. In the opposite case, you will remain in the sack for all eternity, and what's more, you will be soundly beaten every morning."

"Okay, okay!" the devil shouted in rage, "Release me! I will not demand a thing of you."

Once the devil was free, he soared off in his true appearance with a terrible noise and an awful stench. The smith went on to live for a long time, a very long time. Every day he grew a little richer, and gave scarcely a thought to his death, but his hour soon came. After he died, he set off for hell with a jaunty step, full of cheer, whistling and singing, because he thought a person would have more fun in hell than in heaven. When he came to the enormous gate of hell, he knocked on it so violently with the hammer that he had brought with him as a souvenir of the world that he practically staved it in. The devil's grandmother, alone at home eating her soup, put down her bowl. Scowling, she hobbled to the door. "Who goes there?"

"The smith of Rumpelbach!"

"You don't say! So now you show up, you rogue! Do you think you can still fool the devils? Scram. There's no place for you here."

While talking, she piled some cauldrons behind the door to prevent him from easily kicking it in. "Don't give it another thought! Since you're denying me entrance here, I am going to go to heaven."

The smith did an about-face and started off on a long, steep path. When he reached heaven's gate, he knocked very politely, for he had clearly seen that crude manners got him nowhere. Who's there?" asked Saint Peter, the celestial gatekeeper.

"The smith of Rumpelbach!"

"You imagine that we would need rogues here who sign pacts with the devil? Go back down!"

"Now this is very vexing. I would never have thought I would be too bad for hell and too bad for heaven at the same time!" muttered our hero, starting to get steamed, as he headed back the way he came.

When he returned and presented himself at the gates of hell, all the devils large and small who were at home began shouting in unison: "Keep him outside, keep him out, otherwise he might roast us!" The poor smith had to leave and give heaven a second try. He knocked very politely and begged to be allowed in, but Saint Peter pushed him back with even harsher words than the first time. "Let me just get a glance of heaven!" the smith begged.

"Okay, as long as it means we will be rid of you," grumbled the heavenly gatekeeper, cracking open the golden gate.

As soon as the door was ajar, the smith threw his old cap in the air. Saint Peter wanted to get it back for him but he replied, "I'll go fetch it myself." He was therefore given permission to enter so he could get it back. But as soon as he entered, he sat on his cap and jubilantly shouted, "Now I'm on my property!" and nothing or no one could dislodge him.

So where is the smith of Rumpelbach today? In heaven, sitting on his cap and listening to the music of the angels.

Ignaz Vinzenz & Josef Zingerle, Kinder- und Hausmärchen aus Tirol (Innsbruck: Schwick, 1911).

📖 Bechstein 50; Sklarek 44; Róna-Sklarek 30; Haltrich 19.

ATU 330, BP 2, 163–89, EM 12, col. 111–120, Mlex 1033–1036, CPF 1, 346–64.

15. The Devil in the Cask Spigot

Transylvania, Romania

A princess, who was the daughter of a very powerful king, had reached the age of marriage, and her father wished to see her take a husband. Numerous princes and other noblemen presented themselves at court seeking the hand of this charming maiden. But as she was an enthusiastic dancer, she only wanted a husband who could dance for as long as she could. She danced so well and so fast that none of those who dared to try to match her could best her. Many a prince fell down dead in the ballroom, more than one fled with his lungs on fire, and a great number of other noblemen discreetly took their leave when they realized just how formidable a dancer this maiden was.

Months passed and the king, seeing his beloved daughter remaining unwed, had it proclaimed throughout the land that anyone who was capable of besting his daughter at dancing should come forth, and that the first who outdid her would marry her, whatever his rank might be. Then great lords and all sorts of other folk again assembled at the court, of both high and low birth, all feeling they could best the beautiful princess at dancing. The monarch organized a splendid celebration that would last several days, during which they would dance every night by the light of torches and candles.

Dancing had made more than one person ill and weary, and brought about the death of some, but the princess remained without an equal. Suddenly a stranger carved a path through the guests and invited her to dance with him. As soon as she got a good look at him, he filled her with horror and she turned down his request, but, enamored of justice, her father forced her to accept. The princess and her knight were next seen whirling about the room so crazily that it was soon obvious that the maddened dancer had found her master. Indeed, after a moment, almost dead of exhaustion, she asked her companion to excuse her, which he absolutely had no wish to do. The sovereign stood and commanded the stranger to stop, but he paid the king no mind and continued to spin his companion all over the room until, out of breath, her legs collapsed beneath her. He threw the fainted maiden at the feet of the king, sitting on his throne, and said mockingly: "Take back your daughter! I would have the right to take her but I'm not the taker of such a pitiable fiancée. You alone are responsible for this, you old fool! Why didn't you place any restraint on the whims of your child? After all this noisy to-do, only silence will now reign in your palace—for eternity. You and your daughter and the entire court, your palace, the entire city, and everything that lives in it will be petrified. This curse will remain upon you for as long as I remain unvanquished."

The devil's words—for it was definitely him—caused such terror in the king and his entire court that their blood froze and they became petrified. The princess found herself transformed into a statue at the foot of the throne, in front of her father. The evil spell struck the entire palace and the population of the city, until not a thing stirred for miles around.

A thousand years later, a happy-go-lucky fellow was traveling by chance through this region. Everything seemed to be dead; the number of statues he found everywhere stupefied him. Between the houses dense thickets had replaced the charming gardens, and thousands of crows, ravens, and birds of prey were nesting there. Without letting anything worry him, our hero headed directly to the palace, where he fearlessly crossed through its rooms and corridors and opened every door he found. But he did not find a single living soul. He finally found his way to the kitchen, where he saw a roast on a spit with a pile of ashes beneath it. Examining it more closely, he noted that, despite its deceptive color, it was also made of stone. Half amused and half irritated, he broke his staff and made a fire under the spit, telling himself: "Perhaps I could, with the help of God, soften this roast?" The first puffs of smoke were rising up the chimney when an extremely scrawny human leg fell down, which the imperturbable lad pushed to the side without any fuss. But when he saw that the meat, instead of softening, was just turning black, he smashed it on the ground and threaded the leg that had fallen down the chimney onto the spit. A short time later an equally skinny leg followed the same path. "By my faith," he exclaimed, "people eat strange things in this castle. I would have thought they would have chosen larger hams to smoke!" These words had barely left his mouth when an equally scrawny pair of arms, followed by an entire torso to which a head with a very repulsive face was attached, came tumbling out of the chimney. The torso squirmed over to the arms, which it attached to its shoulders, grabbed the closest leg and put it in place, then wrestled the other off the spit and did the same thing. A whole man was now standing before him. Without feeling any fear whatsoever, our hero asked: "Who are you? Answer me, otherwise I am going to take back your half-baked leg."

"May it please my boastful young lord, these legs are mine. I had hung them in the chimney because they were exhausted from my long race."

"You wouldn't think it from looking at them!" teased the young man. "They must have been hanging for a long time."

"That's none of your business," retorted the disturbing character. "Worry about your own legs and not the legs of others. You're a real chatterbox, you know. Beware! Know that I am the devil and the master of this castle; if you wish to be my guest, you must go head-to-head with me."

"Fine," our hero replied, "we will fight tomorrow. Today, I beg you to treat me as your guest in this inhospitable castle, for this long journey has left me hungry and thirsty."

The Prince of Evil accepted and led him into the huge cellars of the palace. The lad opened the spigot of a cask from which flowed the most delicious wine, and he drank his fill. When he turned off the spigot, his wine steward mocked him: "If you don't fight better tomorrow than you drink tonight, there was no point in you coming here."

"If you really want to know how I can drink, let's make a wager to see which of the two of us knows better how to drain a cask of wine dry."

"Ah, that suits me. Stretch out under this barrel, and I will do the same under the other. They contain the same amount of wine down to the very last drop. If you agree, Mr. Braggart, our fight to the death can begin. This way we will avoid having to duel tomorrow."

"This suggestion suits me. Let's do it!"

Each of them got settled comfortably under his cask, the

insouciant, carefree stranger and the devil, perversely leering at his adversary. The lad scarcely opened the spigot, so that the wine only flowed out one drop at a time, and he pretended to swallow huge mouthfuls. Seeing this, the devil flashed a wily smile and shouted: "Go ahead and drink, idiot! You will not manage to drain the cask down to the last drop because it will remain in the spigot. As for me, I promise I won't leave a single drop. I'm going to slip into the spigot and will be able to drain the cask dry this way." He then began to shrink until he could easily enter the narrow spigot, and our happy-go-lucky fellow could only hear the noise of his enormous gulps. Without hesitating, the lad jumped up and closed the spigot the devil had entered, yelling: "Stupid devil, you are done for!" The Prince of Evil began screaming, moaning, and raging horribly but, sparing no concern for him, the lad left the cellar to satisfy his hunger because, of course, he was no longer thirsty. What a surprise he had when he saw the rooms of the palace were now busy with intense signs of life. The countless statues that had amazed him earlier were now alive and racing about in all directions in a joyful stampede. The wild thickets that had housed all kinds of birds were now magnificent gardens festooned with massive flowerbeds that delighted the eyes. The lad also saw servants in fine livery carrying delicious dishes whose aromas filled the air. The main hall was filled with a sweet music to whose sound luxuriously clad people were merrily dancing.

At the far end of this great hall, the king and queen were sitting on their thrones beneath a dais and, at their feet, he saw the princess half sitting, half kneeling on the stairs of the throne. Her head was lying on her mother's knees, and her eyes were full of tears. She looked like someone waking up from a nightmare in which she had offended her parents. However her tear-filled eyes accentuated the charm of the incomparably beautiful maiden even more, so much so that the visitor, paying no more attention to what was going around him and the surprise inspired by his strange garb, could think of nothing but getting closer to the throne. When the sovereign caught sight of him, he called him over and asked who he was, where he came from, and what brought him there. "Sire," the young man replied, "I am incapable of explaining how I came to be here, and I can't even tell if I'm awake or dreaming. Please allow me to tell you all I know of my story." With a wave of his hand, the king bade the entire room to fall silent, and our friend told them all that he knew, ending with the adventure during which he had imprisoned the devil in a wine cask, which inspired the glee of the king and earned him applause from the entire court. Very curious to verify this story, the monarch went at once to the cellar with the storyteller and several members of his household. The cursing and invectives of the imprisoned devil fully convinced him that the young man hadn't lied.

When he returned to the throne, the king again asked for silence and said: "All you who are now present certainly can remember how I had it proclaimed throughout this city and all the land that I would give my beloved daughter's hand in marriage to whoever could dance longer than she could. More than one suitor had already lost his life when a strange character became the winner of this test. However he then rejected my daughter's hand with scorn and cast a horrible curse on all of us. Now this stranger who has appeared here has defeated our enemy and freed us all. It is only right that he weds my daughter and inherits my scepter and crown upon my death. I invite you to pay homage to him here and now." Then the old, easygoing king brought the friendly young man to meet the queen, and he was given the hand of the princess, whose features, which were a thousand times more appealing than any of the ladies of the court at present, did not take long to captivate him completely.

The party continued, the wedding was performed, and from that day on our hero lived with the beautiful princess, who had abandoned her passion for dancing. The young husband never gave a second thought to the fact that he had left his own time to travel one thousand years into the past.

SCHOTT, ARTHUR AND ALBERT, *WALACHISCHE MÄRCHEN*
(STUTTGART AND TÜBINGEN: J.G. COTTA, 1854), 115–21.

16. How Fire Got Inside the Stone

Ukraine

Learn how fire was able to enter stone! One day the devil went to see God and told him: "Lord, it is no surprise that men obey You and pray to You because You heap them with all sorts of benefits. Allow me to govern the world for eight days and we will see if they don't forget You."

"Agreed," Our Lord replied, and the devil got down to work.

All the evil he could imagine he inflicted on humanity, but with no result, for they continued to address fervent prayers to the Creator. "Wait," thought the devil. "If I deprive you of fire, you will have to bow down before me." He gathered everything that was combustible in a gigantic pile that he lit on fire. He kept close watch over the fire to protect it and keep away all those who wanted to light their pipes from it. Men bewailed this state of affairs, and wringing their hands in despair, they prayed to God to bring an end to their distress.

Our Lord summoned Peter and asked him: "My dear Peter, couldn't you steal a little fire from the devil?"

"Why not, but how?" asked Peter in response.

"My dear Peter, what good is it that I founded my Church on you and made you a saint if you don't even know how to fool the devil? Go to a blacksmith's, ask him to forge an iron bar for you, heat it until it is red hot in the devil's fire, and everything you touch with it will catch on fire. Go, my friend, and don't take too long, for men are crying."

"If there is no other solution, then that's what I'll do," said Peter, and set off.

After getting an iron bar, he went to find the devil, and greeted him and chatted with him, stirring the pyre from time to time with his bar, as if he wanted to help the Prince of Evil. Finally, pretending to be totally caught up in the heat of their discussion, he dropped his bar in the blazing fire to heat it until it turned red. When he saw the bar was beginning to turn white hot, he called over to the devil, "Oh well, goodbye, comrade, it is time for me to go."

"Good bye and have a nice trip," the devil replied. "Wait, stop! What is that dirt at the end of your staff?" Taken off guard, Peter remained calm and took off. Suspecting the truth, the devil set off in pursuit. He had almost caught him when God saw Peter from Heaven. Fearing that the iron would grow cold, He shouted down to him: "Hurry and strike the stone!" Peter obeyed, and since that time, fire will come out of a stone when struck by iron.

OSKAR DÄHNHARD, *NATUREGESCHICHTLICHE VOLKSMÄRCHEN,* 4 VOLUMES (LEIPZIG/BERLIN, 1907–1912), VOL. 1, 142.

CHAPTER IV

IN THE DEVIL'S SERVICE

1. The Devil and His Apprentice

Serbia

Once upon a time there was a peasant who had but one son. One day the son said to his father: "Father, what is going to become of us? We cannot go on living this way. I am going to leave to learn any kind of trade. You see what it's like these days; the person plying the most insignificant trade always lives better than a farmworker." His father tried to discourage him from this plan for a long time by showing that a craftsman also has to deal with worry and problems, and therefore he should not leave. But as nothing could dissuade him, the father finally gave his consent, and his son set off in search of work.

As he was cheerfully walking along he came to the edge of a river. While walking along the bank he met a man dressed in green[1] who asked him where he was going. "I'm looking for a master to learn a trade," he replied.

"I'm the one you need," said the man in green. "Come with me and I will teach you a craft, if your heart truly desires it."[2]

Without any hesitation, the lad left with him. While they were winding their way along the riverbank, the master suddenly jumped into the water and began swimming. He then ordered the lad, "Follow me, learn how to swim!" The boy balked, saying he was scared of drowning, but the man replied: "Don't be scared, follow me!" The boy obeyed and heeded his master. Once they were in the middle of the river, the man in green grabbed him around the neck and dove into the depths, for he was the devil. He took the boy down into his lair, where he entrusted him to the charge of an old woman before going back to the surface.

As soon as the old woman found herself alone with the lad, she began to talk to him, "My son, you think that this man is just a master like any other, but you are wrong—he's the devil. He duped me, too, and dragged me down here, even though I was baptized. Listen to me carefully now. I'm going to tell you how to learn his tricks in detail, but if you wish to get free and go back to the Earth, when he asks you if you have learned anything, tell him every time that you still know nothing."

After some time had passed, the devil indeed did ask him: "What have you learned?"

"Nothing yet," he replied.

Three years passed and every time the master asked him, the boy always replied, "Nothing." One day, when the devil repeated his question, the boy replied, "Absolutely nothing. I have even forgotten what I used to know." In a fury, the Prince of Evil declared, "If you have not been able to learn anything until now, you will never learn anything. So go wherever your eyes shall guide you and wherever your feet will carry you!"

The boy, who had mastered all the devil's tricks, rose back to the surface, swam to the bank, and returned home. As soon as his father caught sight of him, he rushed out to meet him and asked: "For the love of God, where have you been, my son?"

"Gone to learn a trade."

Several days later, the annual fair was taking place in a nearby village. The son said to his father: "Let's go to the fair."

"Why should we go there when we don't own anything?"

"Don't worry," his son replied, and they set off. On the way, the lad said, "When we get close, I'm going to change into a handsome stallion,[3] even more handsome than any other horse there, to the surprise of everyone. My master will come to buy the horse and he will pay you whatever price you ask, but make sure you don't give him the bridle![4] As soon as you have the money, take it off me and strike the ground with it." Everything turned out as planned. When the old man brought the horse to the fair, everyone gathered around to admire it, but none dared to ask the price. Suddenly the devil appeared disguised as a Turk, with his head wrapped in a turban and wearing long robes that flowed all the way down to the ground. He came over and asked, "I wish to purchase this horse. How much are you asking for it?" Large as the sum demanded was, the Turk paid it in gold without haggling. But barely had the old man gotten paid when he removed the bridle from the stallion and struck the ground with it. At that moment both horse and seller vanished.[5] When the old man got home with the money, his son was there waiting for him.

When another fair was taking place, the son again invited his father to go there. This time he accompanied him without raising any objections. Once they had drawn close to the market, the boy announced: "I am going to change myself into a shop full of merchandise; there will not be any as beautiful at the entire fair. No one will be able to buy it, but my master will arrive and give you whatever you ask for it. However, make sure that in no case do you hand over the keys to him. As soon as you have received the money, strike the ground with them." Once the transformation was complete, all the fairgoers rushed over to inspect the beautiful boutique. All at once the master appeared, still disguised like a Turk as before, and he asked the old man: "How much do you want for this?" Without balking, the Turk paid the sum asked for, and once the old man had the money in his hand, he struck the ground with the keys, and at that very moment the shop and the seller vanished. The shop turned into a pigeon, and the Turk, who changed into a sparrow hawk, set off in pursuit.

While they were flying past, the king's daughter came out of the palace and saw them. The pigeon immediately landed on her hand and changed into a ring. The sparrow hawk landed and took human form again. He went before the king and urged him to take him into his service. "I will serve you for three years," he told the monarch, "and ask for absolutely nothing in exchange—no food, drink, or clothing—except at the end of that time you will give me the ring that is on your daughter's finger." The sovereign hired him and promised to grant his request. The princess continued to wear the ring, which was her favorite, for while it was a ring during the day, at night it became a handsome young man. He told her, "When the time comes that they try to remove this ring from your finger, don't give it to anyone, and strike the ground with it."

When the three years came to an end, the king sought out his daughter and begged her to give him the ring. Pretending to be angry, she hurled it on the ground, where it exploded into a large number of peas, one of which rolled under the king's shoe. The devil immediately changed into a sparrow that began pecking at the peas at top speed, and he had eaten almost all of them, and was preparing a spell to get the one from under the king's shoe, when that pea suddenly changed into a cat[6] that caught the sparrow and strangled it.

Vuk Stephanovic Karadžić, *Volksmärchen der Serben* (Berlin: Reimer, 1854), 54–60.

ATU 325, BP 2, 60–69, Mlex 1436-1441, EM 14, 1165–1168.

2. Hell's Doorkeeper

Veneto, Italy

Once, a long time ago, an old man had a son who refused to work. One day, he said to his son, "Man is made to work, and everyone has to do something, whatever it may be. Tell me honestly: in the future do you want to work, beg, or enter into someone's service?"

"I choose the last solution," his son replied.

"So be it! And even if it's the devil in person who comes to offer you a position in his service, I will agree to it." Both set off in quest of a position.

On their way they encountered a distinguished gentleman who asked them the purpose of their journey. "I am looking for a job for my son," the father replied.

"Give him to me, for I need a doorkeeper and this boy is large and strong. What salary would you like?" he asked the young man.

"Seven sous."*

"That's too little," replied the man, "I will give you twenty. You will have nothing else to do but open and close the door, but woe to you if you go inside!"[7]

The son began his service and was amazed to see so many people going in this door, but never saw any of them coming out. Among them were many people he knew personally, including the village priest and even his own grandfather. "What can this mean?" he often thought, but it took quite some time before he grasped just who his master was. After a year of this, he had had his fill and asked his master to let him leave. The devil initially refused his request because he didn't want to have to find another doorkeeper, but eventually relented. "Fine, if you absolutely want to leave, come here," he said, leading him to a chest full of gold,

---

*Soldi, one-hundredth of a Fiorino, a florin coined in Florence.

"and take whatever you want as your salary. Let's go, take what you need," he went on to say, when he saw that his servant was hesitating.

"No, I only want what I'm rightfully owed, no more, no less," replied the latter.

Once his master had paid him, he set off and was cheerfully walking along when he met a poor person asking for alms. "Take five sous; I will still have four for tobacco, five for bread, and six for wine." Then he came across another beggar, to whom he gave five sous. "Fine," he said to himself, "I must now divvy up my money differently, for I only have three sous left for tobacco, three for bread, and four for wine," and continued on his way. Then he ran into another beggar. "Farewell, tobacco! A person can also live with five sous for bread!" he exclaimed, laughing, as he parted with another five sous. Then a fourth beggar appeared. "God have mercy! I will no longer have enough in my purse with which to break my fast," he said, giving the poor man his last five sous.[8] A fifth beggar then loomed before him, asking for charity. "My friend," the young man responded, "I've already given away every sou that I had, and I can't guarantee to you that I won't be obliged to beg alms from the next person I meet." Striking his chest, the beggar replied: "I don't need your money. What grace can I bestow upon you?"

"Sir," our traveler said, "from begging a boon to granting a favor is quite a gulf to cross, be careful you don't sprain your ankle! These must be extraordinary graces that you can give away!"

"Ask without racking your brain any longer, and you will see just how extraordinary!" the beggar replied.

"Fine. Give me a rifle whose shot will never miss its target."[9]

"Here you go," said the beggar, pulling it out from under his coat. "Would you like anything else?"

"Yes, a violin that forces everyone to dance as long as I'm playing."[10]

"Here's one. Still something else?"

"Yes, a sack into which everyone I order to do so must jump."[11]

"Here's your sack, and with that I bid you farewell," said the beggar, walking away.

The boy was overjoyed to find himself the owner of these three objects, and longed for a chance to try them out. A beautiful bird flew by him and alit on a pile of wood a good distance away. "Hey!" the young man said, "I'm going to try out my rifle!" He prepared to shoot. Two monks appeared on the path. "You are a funny kind of marksman," said one. "You can't judge size by sight. To reach that bird you would need a cannon; a rifle won't be enough at that distance."

"And yet I'm going to reach it," our hero retorted.

"Very well," said the monk, "if you hit it, I will go fetch it for you completely naked." The young man fired, the bird fell, and he said: "Now keep your promise!" The monk was a man of his word. He took off his robe and went to fetch the bird. But he had barely entered the woods when the young man picked up his violin and began to play. Both monks, one on the road and the other in the woods, started to dance. This was particularly painful for the naked monk, as he was pricked by thorns and yelled horribly.[12] When, like Lazarus, he was completely covered by scratches, the boy stopped playing, but the two monks made their way to the next town and denounced him to the police. They waited for him to arrive, and when he did, they held him for questioning. It was exactly noon and the police chief was having lunch. "Wait until I've finished," he said irritably.

"Gladly!" responded the lad. "With your permission, I'm going to play the violin," he said, and took out his instrument.

With the first strokes of his bow, a strange ballet began in the police chief's dining room: plates, dishes, table, armchair, the chief, his wife, their children, the cat, the servant serving the meal, and a policemen who had come to report all began dancing a Monferino.* The faces of some of the dancers were furious, while the others were frozen in terror. Only once the last drop of soup had escaped the bowl, and the last drop of wine had spilled from the bottle, and the table and chairs had lost several legs, and none of the dancers could keep their breath did he stop playing. But by then the exhausted police chief had lost all desire to interrogate him, and the first thing he could find the breath to say was: "Go to the devil!"

The man left and resumed his journey. The first person he met was his former master. He immediately opened his sack and commanded: "Jump inside!" The devil begged him to let him out, but in vain. "Wait until I've finished lunch," he replied, and carried him to a blacksmith's. When he entered the forge, he told the smith: "I have some iron that needs hammering."

"Take them out," the smith told him.

"No, I want you to strike them in the sack,"

"And I'm telling you that I cannot forge what I cannot see."

So he pulled out his violin and made the smith and his companions dance until they were completely out of breath. "Will you hammer them now?" he asked.

"Of course," they all cried in unison, "even if it's the devil himself in that sack."

"That's precisely who it is!"

"Why didn't you say so? We are going to beat him for your great pleasure. He will not have a single horn left intact, however hard it is."

When the devil had been beaten for an hour, the lad freed him. "You'll get what's coming to you,† you rogue!" screamed the

---

*Popular dance of northern Italy (Lombardy, Emilia-Romagna, Friuli, Venezia Giulia). It has different names: Monferrina di Friuli, Monfrenna Bulgnaisa (of Bologna), Monfrenna Mudnaisa (of Modena), Giardiniera or Window Planter, and Baragazzina (of Baragazza, province of Bologne).
†The Venetian text says, "if you ever fall under my shoe!" (*sotto le mie ciabatte*).

devil as he fled. "If I ever get my hands on you, you will pay what you owe with interest!"

A little farther along, the young man met a pretty and young peasant woman he found quite pleasing. "Come with me," he told her.

"Leave me alone," she replied.

"It would be better for you to accompany me willingly than to be forced to do so."

"Go away, you good-for-nothing," she replied, and pretending to caress him, she give him a good hard slap.

Furiously, he opened his sack and ordered her: "Jump inside!" In his haste, he shut the sack too quickly, so that the peasant girl's head remained outside and she was able to call for help. He fled away with her, but the villagers poured from their houses and set off in pursuit. They were trying to cut him off and were close to succeeding when he threw down the sack so he could take out his rifle. The chase was only ended when he killed one of his pursuers. Out of breath, he came to a small community, where he met an old woman in rags. "Old woman," he asked her, "can you tell me of a place where I could sleep?"

"Follow me," she replied, and led him to a large and splendid palace. Chandeliers illuminated every room and the reception hall held a magnificently set table, but not a living soul was to be seen. He liked the place. He sat down and did justice to the delicate dishes and fine wines. Once he had restored himself, he went to a bedroom to sleep.

At midnight he was awoken and saw that the large room was full of men wearing coats and large wigs. They were dancing and capering with serious expressions on their faces. All at once they vanished and he found himself in a sea of flames. "I am in a real mess!" he thought to himself. "I must try to get away from here." Suddenly men on horses began crossing through the room. "Here's my chance to escape," he thought, and scrambled out of bed and leapt on a horse. But the horse began losing all physical consistency, and the boy found himself sinking deeper and deeper until he came to a door. This was the same door where he had only worked for little more than a year as a doorkeeper, the same door that his successor was now opening for him.

Georg Widter & Adam Wolf, "Volksmärchen aus Venetien," *Jahrbuch für Romanische und Englische Literatur* 8 (Leipzig, 1866): 263–268.

ATU 330 + 475 + 592, BP 2, 423–426, Contes populaires français II, 181–87, EM 6, 1191–1196, Mlex 1189–1191.

3. Apprenticed to the Devil

Finland

Once in a village there lived an old couple who had an only son whom they wanted to apprentice in a suitable profession. One fine morning, the father left with his son for the castle. While on their way there, they ran into the Prince of Evil, who asked: "Where are you going with your son?"

"I am bringing him to the castle so that he may learn a trade."

"Give him to me to be my apprentice."

"Who are you," the old man asked, "and what will you teach him? I want my son to become a blacksmith."

"I'm a smith myself."

"So where do you live?"

"Here," and suddenly a large farm appeared before them.

The father left his son with the devil for five years and returned home. They had agreed that he would not visit him during these five years. When he got back, his wife scolded him for having left his son, and the next morning he returned to the castle, telling himself: "I'm going to fetch him and apprentice him elsewhere."

He reached the spot where they had parted, and searched the entire farm without finding a single living soul.

Five years went by, and with the boy's apprenticeship at an end, the father decided to go fetch him. But the moment he decided to set off, a ball of yarn entered through the window, fell to the ground, and all at once his son was standing there. "Father, when you come to fetch me, they will not let me go. Twelve pigeons will be sent in flight and you will have to guess which of them is your son. I will be the third one leaving from the left. If you pick me, I will go away with you. Otherwise, I will stay there. I am the devil's apprentice." The boy changed back into a ball of yarn and left the same way he came.

The next day, the father returned to the farm. The devil came out to meet him and said, "Did you come to fetch your son?"

"Absolutely!"

"Follow me!" and they left together.

The devil let loose twelve pigeons and told the old man: "If you can find your son among them, you can bring him home."

"I did not give you a pigeon,'" the old man retorted, "now give me back my son."

"If you don't want to look for him, then get out; you will not have him."

"The third one leaving from the left side is my son," replied the old man.

"I'm not going to return him today; you must guess correctly three times," the devil retorted.

The father returned home and told his wife everything. The window was open and suddenly a bullet entered and fell into the entrance hall. It was his son, who told him, "Alas, Father, tomorrow you are going to have to guess again. There are twelve of us boys and we are all the spitting image of each other. I will be the second, starting from the right."

The next day the father returned to the farm and met the

Prince of Evil, who ordered him: "Guess which one is your son!"
He brought him into a room where twelve boys were standing in
a row. The old man looked them over and said, "The second one
starting from the right is my son." But his giving the right answer
held no sway over the devil's mind, and the devil ordered him:
"Come back tomorrow."

The father returned home and once evening fell began waiting
for his son, but in vain. The devil had placed iron chains around
his neck, held by padlocks.

The third day, when the father returned to the farm, he had
no idea how he would recognize his son. The devil came to meet
him and invited him inside. He had twelve stallions brought out
and paraded around. "Very well, do you recognize your son?" the
Prince of Evil asked. Not knowing how to answer, the old man
replied, "My son isn't there." The devil ordered his valet to bring
one of the stallions out of the stables. He was limping and was all
skin and bones, and truly wretched. "Is this your son?" the devil
asked him.

"It's truly him."

"You guess rightly. I would never have dreamed you could.
Take your son and scram!" Inside, the devil was raging because
the old man had outsmarted him.

On the road back, father and son ran into two hunters in front
of whom five wood grouse were flying. They were getting ready to
shoot them but the boy told his father, "I am going to change into
a goshawk and catch them. I will then land on your shoulder, and
you will take the five grouse. When the hunters ask to buy them,
sell them. They will then ask to buy me as well. Sell me, but for
no less than two hundred thalers, and don't sell the gold chains
I'm wearing around my neck." Everything turned out as planned.

The father returned home with the money, but barely had he
gotten undressed when his son appeared. They decided to live it up
and the two hundred thalers were quickly spent. "Father," the boy

said, "I'm going to turn into a fledgling and perch on the whip-cord of your whip. Go sell me at the castle, but for no less than one hundred thalers. But don't sell the whip!" Looking around, the father saw, perched on the whipcord, a small bird singing wonderfully well. He made his way to the castle, while the bird sang the most beautiful melodies. On the way, they met the domain's cook. She brought them before her masters, who were having coffee. When the bird began to sing, their feet began to move despite all their best efforts, and they spilled their coffee and milk.

Two people present stood up to listen to the bird sing while they rocked back and forth. "Approach!" they told the old man. "How much do you want for the bird?"

"One hundred thalers, but I'm not selling the whip."

They acquired the fledgling and the old man returned home, but found his son already there. After some time had passed, they began to run out of money, and the son told his father: "Soon we will have nothing left. I'm going to change myself into a proud charger that you will ride to the castle. You will sell me, but not for less than two thousand thalers."

During this same time, the devil was studying his grimoires to find out where the young man lived and to learn how he was fooling people. He then said to himself: "I'm going to go there and buy the horse." Numerous would-be buyers had come before him, some offering fifteen hundred thalers, some offering quite a bit less. The Prince of Evil approached the father and asked the price of the horse. "I'm selling it for two thousand thalers, but I'm keeping the bridle." The demon handed over the amount requested, leapt on the back of the horse, which was still wearing its bridle, and left. The old man had tried to grab it, but the devil kept it.

The Prince of Evil went to the home of his old sister, who was out. He tied his mount to the edge of the roof so that its front legs couldn't touch the ground. He then stretched out in his sister's bed to rest. When she returned, she saw the horse. "What a handsome animal!" she said. But just look at how he's being treated! I have enough hay to give him some." She untied the horse's front legs and threw him some hay, then went inside and scolded her brother. He asked her, "Did you untie the horse's legs?"

"Yes."

"Well then, he must be a long ways off by now."

They went out to check and saw that the horse had fled. The devil immediately set off in pursuit.

The horse then changed into a bird and the devil into a goshawk, and in those forms flew until they reached the sea. The boy transformed into a fish—a perch—and the Prince of Evil, changed into a pike, set off in pursuit behind him. The perch is a small fish, and it buried itself in the sand. The pike, which is a large fish, swam by without seeing him, and swam until he was exhausted. Mad with rage, the devil returned home empty-handed, leaving the boy behind.

AUGUST VON LÖWIS OF MENAR, *FINNISCHE UND ESTNISCHE VOLKSMÄRCHEN* (IÉNA: EUGEN DIEDERICHS, 1922), 16–21.

📖 Bechstein 26, 51; Sklarek 25; Karadzic 6; Schullerus 25; Haltrich 14; Schott 19 ; Grimm, *Kinder- und hausmärchen* 68 ; Straparola VIII, 4.

ATU 325.

4. The Devil and His Wives

Italian Tyrol

Once upon a time there was a father with three daughters. One day, returning home tired from work, he told the eldest: "Go into the garden and bring me a large radish, for I'm hungry." The young woman obeyed and found a large, beautiful one, but when she tried to pull it up, a voice shouted from out of the ground:

"Pull, pull, but don't cut!" She pulled, but instead of pulling out the radish, it was the vegetable that dragged her down into the depths. She found herself in a large, beautiful meadow, in the middle of which stood a palace.[13] She made her way there and met its inhabitant—the devil! He had her enter and made her his wife. When he gave her all the keys to the palace, he told her: "You can go in all the rooms, but you must never enter the one that can be opened with this gold key."[14] She promised, and he also gave her a fresh rose that she wore as a corsage.

One day, when the devil was away on a trip, she took the keys and visited all the different rooms. Everything in one of them was made of gold, and everything in another was made of silver. A third room was filled with fine lingerie and bright linen. Finally she came to the forbidden door. Paying no mind to her spouse's warning, she opened the door and came face-to-face with a roaring fire, for this was hell. Without her noticing, one tongue of flame licked out and burned the rose on her corsage. She closed the door as fast as she could and went to work in her room. The devil returned soon and asked her: "Did you go everywhere?"

"Yes!"

"Even into the forbidden room?"

"No!" He looked at the rose, and seeing it was burnt,[15] grabbed his wife by the arm and led her to the forbidden room, where he threw her into hell.

Her younger sister, who had come looking for her, also became the devil's wife. The same misadventure happened to her and she, too, was tossed into hell.

In turn, the youngest sister became the devil's wife, and she started looking for her sisters. Because she was very smart, she placed the rose the devil gave her in cool water before entering the forbidden room. When she saw her sisters in hell, she immediately brought them something to eat, then shut the door, put the rose back in her corsage, and went to her room. On his return, the devil immediately looked at the flower, and because it was still fresh, he believed his wife when she told him that she hadn't gone into the forbidden room. But she sought a way to free her sisters[16] as well as herself. "Listen," she said to the devil one day, "wouldn't you allow me to send a little laundry back home?"

"If you like!" he answered.

She went to see her oldest sister in secret, and had her lie down in a basket she had placed in front of the door. The she told her sister, "If you realize that he wants to open the basket, shout: I see you!" She then went to find her husband and asked him, "Who's going to carry the basket?"

"I'll be responsible for it,"[17] he replied.

Satisfied, she added: "But don't open it, I forbid you to do so. Wherever you are, I will be able to see you, you can believe me!" The devil left, but after a short while, his curiosity grew strong, and he put the basket down so he could open it. Grasping what he intended to do, the oldest sister shouted: "I see you!" Frightened, he thought, "Yikes, she can really see me everywhere!" He picked the basket up again, carried it to his wife's house, put it down, and left.

Several days later, his wife sent him to her house with another basket, in which she had hidden her other sister, and then, for the last time, she arranged matters so that the devil also brought her back home.

This is how the three sisters got free. The Prince of Evil later realized that he had been deceived. He almost died of rage, but because he did not have the power to go fetch them, he waited for them to return, and is still waiting today, for all three have been in heaven for a long time.

Il diavolo e le suo sposo, Christian Schneller, *Märchen und Sagen aus Wälschtirol. Ein Beitrag zur deutschen Sagenkunde* (Innsbruck: Wagner'sche Universitäts-Buchhandlung, 1867), 88–90.

📖 Gonzenbach 23; Wlislocki 98; Obert 1; Asbjørnsen 42 (*De tre kongsdøtre i berget det blå*); Hahn 19, 73.

ATU 311, MLEX 317–321, EM 8, 1407–1413.

5. The Prince who Entered Satan's Service and Freed the King from Hell

Lithuania

There was a king who had three sons who had all gone out one day to hunt. One of them got lost while the other two returned home. The prince wandered about the huge forest with an empty belly. Starving and heavy of heart, he wondered how he would ever get out of this situation. Finally at the end of five days, he came upon a clearing in which a palace stood. He entered and visited every room without coming across another living soul.[18] In a large hall, however, he found a table on which a vast quantity of food and drink had been placed. The prince ate his fill, and as soon as he finished, everything on the table vanished. He resumed his exploration of the palace until evening, when he heard someone approaching. It was an old man who asked, "What are you doing in my castle?"

"I got lost in the forest. Could I enter your service?"

"It's possible," replied the old man. "You will poke the fire in the stove, bring in the wood, and take care of the horse in the stable; you will not have anything else to do. I will give you one ruble a day and at meal time you will always find whatever you need on the table." The prince accepted and remained in the home of the old man.

At dusk, his host would fly back to the castle with a flame in his hand. One evening, when the prince had allowed the fire to burn low, his master raced in breathlessly and asked him: "Why isn't the fire burning properly? I got back here just in time," and he gave him a bellows. From that time the prince strove to always do his best.

One day, when the prince was in the stable, the horse began speaking[19] and said, "Approach, I have something to tell you. Take my saddle and bridle out of the cabinet and saddle me. In that vial over there, there is an ointment that you are going to smear over your hair; then take all the wood and fill the stove." The prince did as he was asked and his hair began sparkling and shining as if it was made of diamonds. He then made such a fire in the stove that the castle caught fire. The horse then told him, "Take the mirror, the brush, and the whip in the cabinet, then jump on my back and head out snappily, for the castle is in flames." The prince complied, and they left so quickly that in one hour they had already put three cantons behind them. When the old man returned home and found neither his horse nor his valet, he jumped astride another mount and set off in pursuit of the prince. The horse told the prince: "Look back and see if you can see the devil," for the old man was in fact Satan. When the prince looked back he could see a cloud of smoke. "Gallop!" he ordered his mount. After a little while, the horse repeated the question. "He is really close," the prince exclaimed.

"Throw the mirror!"[20] When the devil's horse passed over it, it collapsed. The old man then returned home, reshod his horse, and resumed his pursuit. He attached less importance to the boy, however, than to the horse he had taken.

In the meantime, the prince had crossed through many lands, and his horse said, "Get down and place your ear on the ground to hear if he is behind us again." The prince obeyed and heard the rumbling of the earth. "He is definitely behind us, the ground is vibrating."

"Climb back on, quick, and let's continue our journey!"

A little later, the horse asked if he could see the devil yet. "I see the flash of a flame far away."

Let's fly!" Then his mount said, "He should not be very far now, look behind you!" The prince turned around and said, "He's right on our heels, the flame is going to attack us!"

"Throw the brush!" the horse commanded, and it immediately transformed into a forest so thick that not even a fly could enter. The devil hit it while traveling at top speed and became stuck in the thickets. He then returned home and got an ax that he used to carve a path through the trees. By the time he brought the ax home and got back on the road, the prince had traveled through several regions. "Prick up your ears," his mount told him. "What can you hear?"

"He's coming like a storm!"

"Let's gallop!"

Looking behind a little later, the prince told the horse: "I already see the fire."

"Throw the whip!" and in the blink of an eye it had changed into a huge river. The devil arrived and began drinking the river with his horse. They drank and drank, and the water level grew lower and lower. Terrified, the prince and his horse could see that all that remained was a small pool. But then the devil and his horse, incapable of drinking one more drop, burst.

The prince moved away from the water and the horse told him, "You can get down now. Satan is dead. Follow the river. You will find a staff with which you will strike the ground. You will then see a door that will open, and the passage will lead us to an underground castle where I will stay. But you should cross through the meadow until you reach a king's garden, where you will ask if he can give you a job. When you have a position, don't forget me." When they were parting, the horse added that he should not let anyone see his shining hair.

When the prince showed up at the king's garden, a gardener asked: "Where are you going?"

"I'm looking for a job," answered the prince, who looked like a poor wretch.

"I can give you one. We need someone to clean the garden lanes and to carry the dirt. You will have a work horse, a salary of two florins* a day, and your meals." The prince accepted and got down to work.

He didn't eat everything he was given, and after a day of work would bring the rest to his horse, who thanked the prince for not forgetting him. One evening, the horse said to him: "Tomorrow, kings, princes, and rich merchants, all bachelors, will arrive at the castle. They will stand in a row in the courtyard. The monarch has three daughters, and each of them will take a diamond apple and throw it. The one at whose feet it comes to rest will be her fiancé. Make sure that you are working in the garden at this time. The apple of the youngest princess, who is also the most beautiful, will roll up to you. Pick it up and stick it in your pocket."

The next day, when all the suitors had assembled, and the king's daughters had thrown their apples, the eldest daughter's apple rolled to the feet of a prince, and that of the middle daughter rolled to a rich merchant, but that of the youngest daughter passed by all the suitors and rolled straight into the garden, up to the feet of the gardener, who picked it up and pocketed it. The king loved his youngest daughter best of all. Nonetheless, he had to grant her hand to the gardener, and the three weddings were performed. But after the betrothals, the gardener and his spouse had to settle outside the court, and he remained what he was.

Time passed and one fine day a number of kings rose up in revolt against the sovereign, who was forced to mount a campaign with his sons-in-law. The husband of the youngest daughter had

---

*These are Polish florins that are worth fifty pennies.

only his workhorse, and the king warned him that he would not be getting another mount. The young man jumped into the saddle, but when he tried to set off, the horse collapsed. He abandoned it and went to fetch his mount in the castle by the river. The horse told him: "Take my bridle and saddle me, go into this room where you will find both clothing and a saber to tie at your waist, and then we will leave." The young man obeyed, and once he was in the saddle, shining like the sun, they flew through the air[21] and landed on the battlefield. As he began striking the enemy with his saber, there were only a handful of soldiers left fighting for the king. But his son-in-law carved the enemy into pieces and gave his father-in-law a victory. When the king and his two sons-in-law realized they were saved, they shouted: "A god has helped us win!" They wanted to keep the young man with them, but he rose into the air and disappeared.

The same scene was repeated several times, but during the last battle the young man's leg was wounded. The king immediately took out his handkerchief, which had his name embroidered on it, bound the wound, and had the prince climb into his carriage to take him back to the castle. But his horse slipped up to him: "Keep me by your side, don't take your hands off my back, and when they wish to take care of me, don't let them do it." While they were traveling, the horse said to saddle him, and they flew away. The war was now over, and everyone was asking who their savior was. "It must be a god," they thought. "If I see him again, even if he's only a man, I will give him one of my lands."

On his return, the prince lay down, and several hairs escaped from beneath his cap. Looking through the keyhole, his wife could see that the room was lit up, and wondered why. She went in and saw that her husband's hair was emitting this light, and that he had his leg bandaged with the king's handkerchief.[22] She rushed to tell her father, and when he recognized the one who had helped him over the course of his campaign, what joy!

The horse, who had lived in the underground palace, changed into a man,[23] and a palace emerged out of the ground. The animal that had been transformed by the devil was the king of this castle, and the prince had freed him from hell. He got his kingdom back, and if he is not dead, he is still reigning even today.

AUGUST LESKIEN, & K. BRUGMAN, *LITAUISCHE VOLKSLIEDER UND MÄRCHEN* (STRASBOURG: TRÜBNER, 1882), 379–385.

📖 Vernaleken 30; Staufe 36; Bechstein 78; Schneller 20; Sklarek 14; Gonzenbach 67; Haltrich 11, 16, 24.

ATU 314.

6. The Devil and His Student

Romania

A peasant, one of the rare ones whose work had actually earned him some money, spent all he had to send his only son to study in a famous city. His son returned once he had finished his studies, but it soon appeared, as is often the case, that he had gotten into the habit of living well with no thought of the cost. Having no more money, his father could only advise his son to work in the fields with him. The young man had little desire to do this, and he implored his father to grant him a final stretch of time to study at the devil's school, which would subsequently allow him to get rich without any difficulty. His father initially refused, but ended up agreeing and accompanied him when the lad set off. They had already walked a while when they met the devil in person, who asked them where they were going. "To the devil's house," they replied.

"To do what?"

"My son," the father responded, "would like to go to the devil's school."

"Give him to me," said the stranger with a laugh, "for I'm the devil."

"What would I have to pay," asked the peasant, "if my son spends a year with you?"

"If, at the end of a year, you recognize your son among all my apprentices, you can take him back without paying a thing; but if you don't recognize him, he will belong to me."

Anxious, the peasant took his son aside and said to him, "After a year of study you will be so changed that I will not be able to recognize you, and you will belong to the devil for eternity."

"Don't worry, Father, I will make a sign that will allow you to easily distinguish me from among the others. I will bend the index finger of my left hand and you will know that I'm the one you're looking for."

This is exactly what happened a year later when the peasant came to fetch his son, but the devil urged him to leave his son for another year, promising to perfect his training. Father and son accepted, and as the same conditions applied, they agreed on a secret sign that would allow the father to recognize his son: he would shake his foot.

Once the year had passed, the peasant went to fetch his son from the school, and the agreed-upon sign once again worked like a charm. But when father and son tried to leave, the devil reiterated his request for an additional year so he could teach him three more magic spells. Father and son put their heads together and the boy said: "When you come to get me at the end of a year, the devil, being careful, will not allow you to enter the school. He will send the students out one by one. So that you can recognize me easily, I will brush past you." Once the peasant was sure of his instruction, he entrusted his child to the devil for the third time, and left.

When the year was up, he appeared at the door to the school and demanded his son. The devil sent out the students one after the other. When his son's turn arrived, the latter lightly brushed against his father, who recognized him at once. Although quite vexed, the devil was forced to give him back.

Once they were back home, the young man said, "I now know how to make a lot of money."

"How will you do it?" his father asked.

"I'm going to transform into a steer, the strength and appearance the likes of which the world has never known, and you will put me up for sale. Many buyers will come to you, but don't sell me for less than two bushels of ducats, and keep the lead rein that is tied to me."

The transformation occurred, and once it was learned that this magnificent beast was for sale a crowd of buyers soon gathered, but none were willing to match the asking price. In the end, a troop of wandering players bought the wonderful animal to exhibit. The peasant went home with the ducats while the players erected a pavilion, adorned the steer, and prepared to display him that very evening before the hastily assembling crowd. In the meantime, this wondrous steer had resumed human form behind the curtain and snuck away. When the curtain was raised, stupor and disarray resulted. "Imposters, imposters!" those in the crowd shouted at the top of their voices. Everyone, spectators and players, demanded their money back, while the crowd continued to mock everyone. This grew so riotous that the authorities had to come to restore order.

From then on, father and son lived a life of ease thanks to the ducats, and didn't look to earn any other money so long as the ducats held out. Once the money ran out, the son said: "I am now going to change into a horse that has no equal throughout the land. Among the buyers will be the devil, but don't sell me for less than at least six bushels of ducats, and don't forget to take off my bridle so I can come back." Immediately a steed of extraordinary beauty was standing before the peasant, who the next day took it to the fair in the neighboring village. Many buyers approached him, but a scant few were capable of paying this exorbitant price. Finally, as the son had predicted, the devil appeared. He bought the horse, paying the six bushes of ducats, but insisted absolutely on keeping the bridle, saying he would not complete the sale if he could not have it. The peasant, who was already in possession of this pile of gold, heeded the advice of the spectators, who told him, "For such a large sum, the bridle means nothing," and he yielded to the devil's wishes. Enchanted, the devil returned home and began mistreating the animal instead of feeding it and caring for it properly.

A short time later, the devils were celebrating a wedding, and the horse's new owner sent his son with instructions not to feed or water his mount during the journey. Instead of quietly riding, all the imps heading for the wedding were forcing their steeds to gallop, as is generally the case when young men find themselves in this kind of situation. However, they watered their horses when they were crossing a stream, except for the little devil whose father had forbidden it. His comrades then advised him to do as they were doing, "otherwise you will not be able to keep up with us on your thirsty nag, and you will bring dishonor on us all." This made the young devil decide to water his mount. But barely had the horse swallowed a mouthful of water when it changed into a gudgeon, and the imp, to the great surprise of his companions, found himself in the water while the fish flitted away.

His father, who, thanks to his knowledge, realized what had happened at once, arrived at top speed and began swimming in pursuit of the fugitive. The gudgeon had gained a decent lead and had met another fish, whom he had asked, "Dear friend, if you run into a devil, tell him, if he asks, that you are coming out of the depths and haven't seen me." The fish promised and kept his word. When the devil questioned him, he said, "I am coming from the depths and haven't encountered even the smallest gudgeon." The devil reversed course and swam back to where he had started, but not finding the gudgeon, set off again in the other direction as quick as lightning, and was soon behind the lad who had changed himself into a gudgeon. When the young man saw that his enemy was close, without wasting any time, he changed into a beautiful gold ring, jumped onto the finger of a princess who happened to be washing her hand on the bank at that very moment, and said to her: "I beg you, most beautiful of princesses, don't give me to the devil!" Barely had he stopped speaking when to the great surprise of the maiden the devil appeared, demanding the ring she had on her finger, which belonged to him. She impertinently shot back, "The one on my finger has been there for a long time and belongs to me. I don't have the one you're asking for." She then turned her back on him and returned to her father's palace.

The devil, who absolutely coveted this ring, followed her and pressed his demands again to the king, to whom he promised all possible wealth and treasures. In the meantime the ring had told the princess: "Most dear princess, don't give me to the devil until he has built a golden bridge around which wondrous trees are growing, and at whose center is a gold fountain. Then tell him you will give him back the ring, but instead of placing it in his hand, throw it on the ground." She carefully noted what he had told her, and when her father urged her to obey the devil, she did what they had agreed upon.

Barely had she made her request when in the castle's courtyard a gold bridge arose. It had a fountain at the center and was bordered on each side by verdant trees. The king, queen, and princess went down to contemplate this wonder more closely, and to give the devil, who was following them, the ring he wanted. When all three reached the fountain, at the moment the princess had to keep her promise, she dropped the ring and it changed into a myriad of seeds that spread everywhere. When he saw this, the devil changed into a rooster and began pecking at them and swallowing them as fast as he could. But one of them fell into the princess's shoe and transformed into a lapwing, which flitted around and around the rooster. Because it was more skilled at flying than the rooster, it targeted its eyes and skull with its beak, and after several mighty pecks, the devil left this life. The lapwing then took human form and a handsome young man appeared before the stupefied eyes of the king, queen, and princess. She was all the more overjoyed at having had the courage to give her aid to such a handsome stranger. The entire court was dying of curiosity to learn the story of this singular young man, and invited him into the castle to hear it. He complied readily with their desire and spoke of the devil's school that he had attended, then how he had consistently escaped the devil's clutches, and all the adventures related in this tale. The king found no reason to oppose his daughter's marriage to a peasant's son who was smarter than the devil. And the young man and the princess made no objection! People say that the king was always satisfied with his son-in-law for as long as he lived because, on every occasion, he offered him the best advice. On the king's death, his son-in-law mounted the throne, and reigned for many years with his beloved wife in the most total bliss.

ARTHUR AND ALBERT SCHOTT,
RUMÄNISCHE VOLKSERZÄHLUNGEN AUS DEM BANAT
(BUKAREST: KRITERION, 1975).

Bechstein 26, 51; Sklarek 25; Karadzic 6; Schullerus 25; Haltrich 14; Schott 19; KHM 68; Straparola VIII, 4.

ATU 325, BP 2, 60–69, EM 3, 655–657.

CHAPTER V

A VISIT TO HELL

1. The Sergeant Who Went Down into Hell

Portugal

In a certain place there once lived a sergeant who was a very skilled and clever man. He won the admiration of a rich merchant, who obtained his discharge from the military and hired him into his service. The merchant had three daughters, and the sergeant fell in love with one of them. But this merchant was a very jealous man and never let his daughters out of his sight. Because he held the young man in high esteem, he brought up the subject of marriage himself. Things followed their course and one day it happened that a play was being staged at the theater, which the young women wished to see. They therefore begged the sergeant to speak to their father, as he was the only one who could get their father's permission. "I will permit you to go with the sergeant on the condition that by the last stroke of midnight you will be back home." They all promised and left. Shortly before midnight, the young man warned his fiancée and her sisters that it was time to leave. "Let's stay just a little longer, just a little longer," they begged, and when midnight sounded they were still far from home.

As soon as the sergeant knocked on the door, the merchant opened it and began yelling: "So this is how you obey me! Gather your things together at once, and leave this house."

"For such a trivial thing, and even when I am about to wed your daughter?"

"There is only a single way," replied the father, "for the wedding to take place."

"What is it?"

"Go down into hell and bring me back three rings that the devil is wearing, two under his arms and one in his eye." The young man thought this was impossible, but what else could he do other than simply go away?

In the first place he stopped, he let it be known that if anyone had a message to send to hell, he would transmit it the next day. This caused a sensation and even made its way to the ears of the king. He summoned the sergeant and asked him, "How do you reckon on getting into hell?"

"Your Majesty, I don't yet know the way. I'm looking for it, but I'm going down there whatever may befall me."

"Fine. If you meet the devil, ask him if he knows anything about a very valuable ring that I lost. I'm still grieving its loss."

The young man continued on his way and made the same declaration in another city, whose king summoned him and said: "I have a daughter who is suffering a serious illness whose cause none can determine. If you find your way to hell, I would like you to learn how my daughter might be cured."

Still searching for hell, the sergeant continued his route and reached a crossroads. On one of the roads human footprints could be seen, and on the other that of sheep. He gave the matter some thought and eventually took the road with the human footprints. Further along this road, he ran into a white-bearded hermit who was saying his rosary. He told him: "You did right to choose this path, because the other leads to hell."

"That is exactly what I've been seeking for such a long time!" The young man told the hermit his story and the other, taking pity on him, said: "If you want to go to hell, go there, but always carry some of these rosary seeds, because before you get there you will have to cross a dark river, and you will need a bird to carry you to the other side. When he tries to drop you in the river, toss one of these seeds down his gullet. What happens after that, I have no idea." And with that, he went on his way.

Once he reached hell, the young man became very frightened and hid inside an empty oven he found. While he was scrunched up inside it, an old woman came by and spotted him. "A lad here? My poor lamb, aren't you a handsome one! When my son sees you he will certainly kill you. Why have you come?" The young man told her the whole story of his woes. Compassionately, the old woman told him: "Stay hidden here, because I don't know when my son is coming back. He's at the side of the Holy Father, who's on his deathbed, and he would like to carry off his soul." The young man asked her if she would be able to get answers to the questions he had been given. It was right then that the devil returned, all out of breath. The old woman quickly hid her visitor and said to her son, "Come give me a snuggle." He did so and fell right to sleep. The old woman quickly extended her claws and took the ring from under one of his arms, With a start, the devil cried out: "What's going on?"

"Alas my son, I fell asleep and accidently struck you in my slumber. I was dreaming about a king who lost his ring and never found it again."

"That's a true dream," her son replied. "The ring can be found beneath a stone near the fountain in the garden." The Prince of Evil fell back to sleep and the old woman furtively removed the second ring. The devil woke up with a start and his mother said to him, "Calm down, son. I nodded off and was dreaming about a princess that no medicine can cure."

"That's also true! Her illness comes from the toad that is hiding in her straw mattress."

The devil again went back to sleep. But this time it was quite difficult to remove the ring from his eye. She finally got it out with a roasting spit. The pain and irritation this provoked caused him to jump up and down all the way to the door. The old woman gave the young man the rings and shared the answers she had gotten from her son. She then summoned the bird so it could return him to earth.

He first returned the rosary to the hermit, and then went to the home of the king who had lost his ring.* The king richly rewarded him when the ring was recovered from under a stone. He then went to the court of the sovereign whose daughter was ill, and told him where the toad was hiding. The princess became better at once, and the monarch asked him what he wanted for his reward. "I would like Your Majesty to grant me his power for eight days." The king then had it proclaimed that the lad would rule for eight days.

He immediately went to his would-be father-in-law's village and ordered that this individual present himself before the king in half an hour, as they had something to discuss. The merchant started off, but took an hour to get there. "I could put you to death because you disobeyed me by arriving late," said the young man.

"Alas, milord, I was not late on purpose."

"Fine! But why didn't you forgive that poor sergeant that you drove away from your home earlier?"

The merchant then recognized his daughter's fiancé in the man he thought was the king. His daughter had not stopped weeping since he'd sent him away. He acknowledged his mistake

*The storyteller doesn't respect the tale's chronology.

and got down on his knees and repeatedly asked for forgiveness. The young man then gave him the devil's rings, and that very day married his beloved, for whom he had gone all the way to hell.

"O SARGENTO QUE FUOI AO INFERNO," IN TEÓFILO FERNANDES BRAGA, CONTOS TRADICIONAES DO POVO PORTUGUEZ, COM UM ESTUDO SOBRE A NOVELLISTICA GERAL E NOTAS COMPARATIVAS (PORTO: LIVRARÍA UNIVERSAL DE MAGALHÃES & MONIZ-EDITORES, 1883), 130–134.

2. The Abduction of the Princess

Austria

A long time ago there lived a powerful monarch whose wife was as rich as she was beautiful. She gave birth to a little girl, but with the day of baptism fast approaching she could not decide on a godmother. On the eve of the ceremony, a white lady suggested herself, and the parents accepted her offer joyfully, thinking that this magician would endow their daughter in every possible way. Their hopes were not disappointed as she proved to be most generous, but she forbade the parents from allowing the child to leave her room before her twelfth birthday, in order to avoid misfortune.

The young girl was already eleven when, one beautiful summer day, she asked her father if she could go hunting with him. Unable to resist her insistent requests, the king yielded to his daughter. But they had barely gotten outside when a man riding a splendid winged horse grabbed her and flew away with her. The king vainly shouted for help, but the horse was already so high in the sky it was no longer visible. He went to find his wife and told her of the tragedy, which plunged them deep in sorrow.

One evening the white lady, who had learned of the misfortune that had befallen her godchild, visited the king to console him, but she was powerless with respect to the devil that had carried off his daughter. She gave the royal couple some comfort by telling them their child could still be saved if a young man under twenty dared venture to hell to find the three waters there: that of life, that of beauty, and that of love. This would allow him to not only free their daughter, but two other princesses as well.

The king then had it proclaimed throughout the kingdom that whoever rescued his daughter from the hands of the devil would become her husband. For a long time no one came forth. Finally one day a peasant said he would try. The king gave him a handsome sum of money so that he would not lack for anything, and he set off on his journey with a determined stride. When he had already been traveling for some time, he came across an old woman with a very wrinkled face and asked her: "Is this the right road to hell?"

"What does that matter to you!?" she replied in a grating voice. "Abandon your plans, for the devil is an ogre and he will certainly devour you if he sees you."

Because she was unable to dissuade the young man, she gave him a rod, saying, "If you shake this in your right hand, the wild animals guarding the entrance to hell will not be able to do anything to you." He thanked her and resumed his journey.

He met a rooster, who also asked him where he was going. "I'm going to hell to save the princess." The rooster advised him against it, but when he saw he could not convince him, he invited him home to quench his thirst and satisfy his appetite. While he was there, the rooster gave him three feathers and told him, "Stick these in your cap and the infernal beasts will not attack you." The peasant boy thanked him, and feeling bucked up, took to the road again.

A little farther, he met another old woman. "Is this the right road to hell?" he asked her.

"Yes," she replied, giving him a large sword that would prove useful. Then she added: "At the entrance to hell two snakes will

ask you who you are. Don't answer, and hit their heads with the
rod. If they still refuse to let you in, put one of your three rooster
feathers on the rod and tickle the two reptiles' tongues with it.
They will flee away hissing." The peasant thanked her and quickened his pace, so as to reach hell before nightfall. Once he got
there, he followed the old woman's instructions to the letter, and
everything turned out as he'd been told.

He entered a long, poorly-lit corridor full of horrible monsters,
dragons, and serpents. He could only keep them away by hitting
them with the rod. The passageway led into a large garden, in the
middle of which stood a castle whose walls were richly decorated
with gold and silver. The peasant asked himself if he should enter,
and finally worked up the resolve to do so. He had already crossed
through several luxuriously furnished rooms when he reached a
room from which he could hear the voices of women. He went
in and found three princesses, who were stupefied to see him. He
explained the reason of his coming, which gave them some solace,
but they were fearful that he could not achieve his purpose. "The
devil," they said, "spends his time abducting young girls; he has
held us prisoner for a long time, and he will not spare you." They
agreed that each of them would take turns hiding him under the
straw mattress of their beds at night, as the devil was busy during
the day going about his business.

When night fell, one of them hid him beneath her bed. She
had barely done so when the devil entered in the form of a dragon
and bellowed: "I smell human flesh! If you don't tell me where it
is, I'm going to eat all three of you."

"Oh," said the first princess, "it's the freshly slain game in the
next room that is giving off that odor."

Mollified, the devil went to lie down and slept through the
night. In the morning, after he left, the peasant crawled out from
his hiding place, and the princesses showed him all that there was
to see in the castle. When night fell, the second princess hid him

in her bed. When the devil returned he roared in rage: "I smell human flesh!"

"Stop and think," one of the princesses replied, "that's a calf that was just slaughtered; that's what's giving off that odor."

The third night, the last princess gave him a hiding place, and when the devil entered to say he could smell human flesh, she told him, "It's only the scorched flour of some burnt soup." Pacified, the Prince of Evil went to bed, and left again the next day to go about his usual occupations.

Because the peasant had spent the night with each of the princesses, they were now freed, and they all fled together. He had stolen the three waters of life, beauty, and love, and gave one to each of the princesses. They got into one of the devil's carriages and hitched it to his favorite horse, which had wings. At the gate, two serpents asked who they were, but they didn't respond. After they had traveled a good distance, they came to a forest, where they got lost. Night had fallen and they could find no way out. They eventually caught sight of a large building, but the princesses saw immediately that it was the dwelling of the devil, and they thought all was lost. The peasant hid the princesses in a nearby cave, and went to the house by himself with hopes of slaying the devil with his sword. When he reached the door he saw a snake keeping watch. "Is the devil here?" he asked it. The serpent nodded but would not let him enter. He brandished his sword and decapitated it. Immediately the devil appeared in person and a tough battle broke out between them. The peasant ultimately prevailed and rushed to share the good news with the princesses, who were thrilled.

They set off again and soon came to the hut of the old woman who had given the peasant lad the sword. She asked the young man to give her a few drops of the water of life. She used it to moisten her face and transformed into a young woman. At that same time thunder and lightning rent the sky and in place of the hut stood a splendid castle. The young woman thanked him for freeing her, and gave them the warmest of welcomes to her palace.

The next day they resumed their journey, and by that evening had reached the home of the rooster, who congratulated the peasant lad for freeing the three princesses. The rooster asked him for help removing the curse that weighed on him. To do this, he had to put the three feathers the rooster had given him back in the spots where they were missing. Barely had he finished when a violent explosion echoed throughout the area, and in the place where the rooster's wretched home had stood there was now a castle. The rooster himself had turned back into a prince. He thanked the peasant, who then resumed his journey with the three princesses. They soon came to the hut of the old woman who had given him the rod. He freed her by touching the four corners of the house with the rod. A magnificent palace suddenly emerged, and the old crone was once again a young princess.

The next day they came to the royal palace. You can well imagine the joy of the king! A wedding was organized immediately and the white lady was invited to attend. As for the two other princesses freed by the peasant lad, they went home to their parents.

Theodor Vernaleken, Kinder-und Hausmärchen in den Alpenländern (Vienna: W. Braumüller, 1863), 107–113.

3. The Student Who Went to Hell and Heaven

Lithuania

A skilled blacksmith was heading to the city one day. While crossing the forest, because it was foggy, he became lost. He wandered for two days without finding a way out. Anxiously he set off again on the third day and met a rustic devil who asked him where he was going. "It has been three days since I got lost," he replied, "and I still cannot find my way out of this forest."

"If you promise to give me something that you did not leave behind when you left," the devil said, "I will help you get out of the woods right away and show you the return path."

The smith asked himself, "What didn't I leave at the house?" and as he had no answer for that question, he made a pact with the devil and, at the devil's request, signed it. The Evil One then guided him safely out of the forest, and a short time later our hero was back home.

He had barely stepped into the courtyard and was still sitting in his cart when servants came to tell him that a stork had brought him a boy. His horror at this news was so great that he fainted because, according to the pact he had signed, the child belonged to the devil. When he came back to his senses, he thought, "If my child doesn't die soon, it may be possible to pry him out of the devil's claws by cunning." So he did not mention the pact to anyone.

Once his son had grown old enough, he was sent to school, then high school, and finally to the university. During this time when he was at school, his father said to him one day, "Alas, my child, I have to confess that I promised you to the devil at the time of your birth, and have been obliged to send him a text stipulating that you will go to hell after your death."

"Father," his son replied, "don't worry, I have no fear of the devil or hell. You did well to warn me. I'm going to go to hell and force the devil to give me this pact."[1]

Several days later he set off. After walking for some time, just as night was falling he came to a small house at the edge of the forest, far from any village. Exhausted, he went in and found a little old lady whom he asked for hospitality. "My dear sir," she replied,

"I would happily welcome you, but I have six boys, all brigands. When they come home, they will kill you." As he was keeling over from exhaustion, he replied, "Maybe they will spare me, as I am a poor student and have no money." The old woman agreed to give him shelter, and urged him to slip under the wood stove so her sons would not find him. When they came back, the oldest one asked: "Mother, is there a stranger here?"

"I wouldn't know anything about that," she responded. Now shouting, the brigand continued, "Stop your joking! I smell a man. Go fetch him and bring him here."

"Leave him alone, he's a poor student who begged and begged me for a place to sleep. He has made a long journey and is completely exhausted." The monster roared even louder, like a lion: "Bring him right now!" She went to fetch the boy, who hauled himself out from under the stove and went into the other room.

The brigand leader immediately demanded, "Where are you going?"

"To hell."

"That's fine. Once you have settled your business there, go to heaven—it's not a long way from hell—and ask Our Lord if a great and terrible brigand such as myself can atone and find salvation, and what penitence He would impose on me."

The student promised to get this information, and his life was spared. The next morning he was given breakfast plus some food for the journey. After warmly thanking all of them and bidding them farewell, he set off again.

He finally made it to hell after a long, long walk. The door was closed, of course, but it was opened to him at once after he knocked. Inside he found a large number of devils, as well as Beelzebub tied by a very strong iron chain to a solid oaken post. In his rage he was struggling, stamping his feet, and shaking his chain so loudly that all of hell was in a commotion and all the devils were trembling. But the student just stood there, impervious. After a little while, Beelzebub asked him: "What do you want here?"

"I've come to fetch my pact."

"Who has this pact," Beelzebub asked.

"A devil."

"When and how did this happen?" The student told him the whole story. Furious, Beelzebub summoned all his servants before him. "Who has this student's pact?" All denied they had it. He issued a second summons and many more devils appeared, but not a one had the pact. He then issued a third summons and, finally, a lame devil came limping before him—he was the one who had it! Beelzebub ordered him to give it to the student but he refused. The others grabbed him and tossed him into the boiling pitch, with no better result. They whipped him with iron rods, but he stubbornly resisted. They threw him in the flames without success. As they were out of ideas, Beelzebub thought up a punishment. In a nearby corner of hell there was a bed intended for the brigand at whose house the student had found shelter. It was full of pointed awls and sharp knives. Beelzebub ordered the other devils to throw the recalcitrant devil on it and to turn him over and over. Unable to tolerate this torture and mad with rage, he gave the student the pact. Once he had it safely in his possession, the lad hastened to leave hell and make his way to heaven, as he had promised the brigand.

Once there, Our Lord asked him what he wanted. "During the course of my journey to hell to recover my pact, I was luckily given shelter by a brigand who demanded I ask you the following question: will he be able to atone for his transgressions, and what penitence will you impose on him?"

"This: he must plant the thick apple wood club with which he has killed so many people, and water it every day until it sprouts branches bearing apples.[2] Then his penitence will be achieved."

On his way back home, the student brought this response to

the brigand,[3] who thanked him warmly and gave him lodging for the night. The next morning he supplied the boy with provisions, and promised to begin his penitence at once.

The student got home safe and sound, and the joy of his parents only grew on learning that, thanks to his cunning and daring, their son had gone to fetch the pact in hell and brought it back home. His father immediately recognized the document that he had given to the devil in the forest.

Later the student became a priest and, after a number of years had passed, was making a journey that took him, by chance, through the forest where the brigand's house was located. While slowly going by, lost in his thoughts, he suddenly caught a whiff of a delicious aroma and ordered his coachman to stop. The smell grew stronger once the coach had come to a halt. "Go see what is making that smell," he ordered his coachman. "It must be an apple tree covered with delicious apples. Try to find it and pick as many fruits as you can."

The man quickly found the tree, but when he tried to pick an apple, the branches straightened up and he couldn't pick a thing. He returned to explain to the priest: "I found the apple tree but couldn't get a single fruit. Every time I tried, the branches would move out of reach."[4] Dismayed, the priest remembered the brigand and his penitence. He hopped out of the coach and headed toward the tree. Looking around, he saw the silhouette of the brigand kneeling beneath the tree. He spoke to him and received this reply: "I have completed my penitence. I would now like absolution so I can finally go beyond." The priest put on his alb and approached him to take his confession. Every time the brigand confessed a sin—plop—an apple fell on the ground. Only two were left at the top of the tree. Seeing this, the priest said, "Two sins remain that you haven't confessed. If you hide them from me, you will go to hell." The brigand confessed: "I killed my father and my only sister." Immediately the last two apples fell to the ground. The priest realized that his confession was complete, and he told him that all his sins were forgiven. He then gave him a kick, and the brigand collapsed into a pile of dust as if he were a puffball.* The priest realized he had been saved and resumed his journey.

AUGUST SCHLEICHER, *LITAUISCHE MARCHEN, SPRICHTWORTE, RÄTSEL UND LIEDER* (WEIMAR: BÖHLAU, 1857), 75–79.

---

*A mushroom that transforms into a sack full of brown powder when it is old.

CHAPTER VI

THE DEVIL AND
THE CHURCH

1. The Gypsy and
the Three Devils

Transylvania, Romania

One day Christ, Saint Peter, and Saint John were traveling through many lands to see how the world was doing. One day they came to the home of a gypsy and asked for hospitality. Only his wife was present, as her husband was at the inn. "I would gladly let you stay here," she told them, "but my husband will mistreat you when he returns."

"That should not be so terrible," Our Lord said. "We will find a corner to sleep in and he will hardly notice us."

The mistress of the house could not long refuse to give them shelter. She prepared straw bedding and the three travelers lay down, Christ first, John in the middle, and Peter against the wall.

When the gypsy returned home, full of drink, he began raging and fuming, and beating his wife. "You think I'm drunk, you liar!"

"But I haven't said a thing!"

At this moment he caught sight of the three men lying in the straw. "Snake, who are these men?"

"They are weary travelers."

"By a thousand thunders, can't they sleep in the street?"

Leaving his wife, he began hitting the first one he came to, who was Christ. Our Lord didn't stir. When the travelers took their leave in the morning, the gypsy had sobered up and excused himself for smacking them. "I didn't mean to, but when I'm lit up, I have to punch someone."

"Don't get worked up about it, no one is above reproach," Christ replied good-naturedly, and they left.

The next year, Christ came back with his two disciples. The gypsy wasn't home but was at the inn, as was typical when he had some money. This time, Christ slept in the middle. When, dead drunk, the gypsy got home, he flew off the handle and hit his wife, and when she told him the three poor travelers were there again, he left his wife alone and started beating the middle sleeper. "It's his turn now," he told himself, but it was again Christ whom he was hitting. The next day he apologized like before and Our Lord again said, "Don't get worked up about it, no one is above reproach."

At the end of another year, our three travelers returned to the gypsy's house. This time, Christ slept next to the wall. When their host came home much the worse for drink, he decided to beat the third person. "Everyone will get his fair share of smacks," he said to himself, but once again it was Christ who bore the brunt. When they were leaving the next morning, the man again apologized for his bad manners and said he was not truly bad at heart. Seeing that he was basically good, Christ said to him: "Make three wishes."

"I wish to have a purse that never gets empty,[1] a mirror that has the power to immobilize whoever sees their reflection in it and that only frees the captive when I say so,[2] and finally a pear tree in front of my house that always bears fruit and is made so that whoever climbs into it cannot climb down without my help."[3]

"Let it be so!" Christ said, and then he set off with John and Peter.

The next day the gypsy was delighted to see that his wishes had been granted. "I have everything I asked for—it's the sweet life for me from now on!" From that day on he spent every day at the inn, living like a king. He ate pork every day and drank sweet Rosoli* from morning to night. But when it came time for him to die, the devil showed up and shouted, "Okay my fine fellow, you are mine now. Get up and follow me."

"One second, let me get my stuff. While I'm busy, take some time to look in this mirror at how handsome you are."

The Evil One did just that, for he thought he was quite attractive and looked at himself in a mirror whenever he could. During this time, the gypsy made his way to the forge, took some red hot tongs, then went back and used them to grab the devil's nose, stretching and burning it. Unable to move a muscle, all the wretched devil could do was howl in pain. The gypsy eventually let him go, and he took off as fast as his feet could carry him, just happy to have escaped with his life. Our hero then said to himself, "It will be a long time before he comes back to visit me."

When the devil arrived in hell, all out of breath, he told his brother and father of his misadventure. Seeing the state of his nose, they didn't doubt for a moment that he was telling them the truth. "Poor wretch," his brother said to him. "Wait and see how it's done. I'm going to go fetch him and teach him a lesson!" He went to the gypsy's home, and without even a hello, accosted him brusquely from the street outside, because he didn't want to go inside and see himself in the mirror. "You are mine! Follow me."

"Right away," our hero replied. "I just need to gather some foodstuffs for the long journey." He then came out with a large

---

*A liqueur made from cherry juice or sometimes elderberries or blackcurrants.

coal sack before telling the devil: "Be a good guy and fill this sack while I get dressed for the trip." The devil agreed, for he had his eye on this tree's beautiful pears and yearned for them. The gypsy went back to the forge and took a long iron bar, sharpened one end, and heated it white hot. Returning home, he used it to prick the devil, who began howling. He continued climbing higher and higher in the pear tree to escape his tormenter. But the gypsy leaned a ladder against the tree and continued poking the devil's side. The devil made his way to the top of the tree and perched on a branch that broke. He fell with a thud and broke his leg. However, he jumped up quite briskly and, still howling, was off like a shot back to hell. Maliciously, his brother told him, "He got you, I warned you." Without stopping his moaning, the other showed him his broken leg while pressing his hands to his riddled sides. Their father didn't know what to say and ended up sighing, "He must be one hell of a fellow, I would like to meet him," but didn't seem in any hurry to make his words a reality.

From then on, the gypsy led a pleasant and carefree life. When he felt death drawing close, he ordered that his leather apron, his nails, his hammers, and his tongs be placed close to him. After he died, he presented himself at heaven's gates and knocked. Saint Peter arrived carrying his keys and opened them, but when he saw the gypsy, he shouted, "You have no business here because you led a life of sin," and he slammed the gates in his face. Keeping a low profile, the man repeated his request and said, "I'm prepared to do all your smithy work for nothing," and put some nails that had fallen out back into heaven's gates. But Saint Peter would not hear of it. The gypsy's only option was to go to hell to take his chances there. "At least," he consoled himself, "fire will be free and I will be able to continue to work." When he got to the door to hell, he grabbed his hammer and knocked. The young devil with the lengthened nose came and glued his eye to a crack in the door. He immediately recognized the horrible fellow and, terrified, began screaming: "He is here! He is here!" At these words the devil who had climbed the pear tree also started running, which frightened the old devil so much, he imitated the example set by his two sons. They all hid in hell's deepest depths while the gypsy continued to knock on the door, louder and louder. "I would still like to get a look at him," the old devil said, and although his sons tried to hold him back, his curiosity compelled him to go.

He cracked open the door and stuck his nose out. Crack!

The gypsy seized the end of his nose with his tongs. The old devil quickly slammed the door shut, but caught his beard in it. Despite all his efforts he was unable to free himself. His sons didn't dare come help him, so the old devil perished miserably. Since that time, he is never mentioned; only his sons are, the long-nosed devil and the lame devil.

The gypsy eventually got bored standing in front of the door to hell, and returned to the gates of heaven, but Saint Peter remained unyielding. "Fine. Since they don't want me in either heaven or hell, I'm going back to Earth. Whatever anyone says, it's a lot better!" And this is why the gypsy is still here. If he has money he goes to the inn and if he doesn't, he earns it playing the violin or forging nails for planks and shoes with his hammer.

JOSEF HALTRICH, *DEUTSCHE VOLKSMÄRCHEN AUS DEM SACHSENLANDE IN SIEBENBÜRGEN* (VIENNA: VERLAG VON CARL GRAESER, JULIUS SPRINGER, 1856), 161–67.

ATU 791.

2. The Deacon Was a Devil

Bulgaria

Once upon a time there was a bishop who didn't know that his head deacon, whom he trusted completely, was a devil. This devil deacon wrote in the prelate's books that bishops were allowed to marry. One day when he was reading, the bishop stumbled upon this passage, and got engaged a short time later. When it was learned that the prelate was getting married, the faithful brought him gifts. One brought a goat, another a turkey, and a third a hen, each according to their means. Having nothing else to give, a poor old man took a young cockerel and set off to bring it to the bishop. Night caught him mid-journey and he stopped near a pear tree, placed the cockerel in the tree, and stretched out beneath it. When midnight came, it brought devils with it who climbed into the tree. One of them noticed the man sleeping under it. They put their heads together wondering who he might be. The old man heard them and with his teeth chattering in fear, he played dead. The devils kicked him and pushed him and pulled him in every direction. Whatever they did, he didn't move a muscle. Believing he was truly dead, they abandoned him. Once they had all climbed into the tree, their leader, who, in addition to the tail[4] they all had, also had horns,[5] took a seat surrounded by his fellows. Each of them told what he had done and was rewarded in accordance with his actions. One said, "I sowed discord between two brothers who started fighting each other in their field." Another said, "I tricked neighbors into quarreling," and so on. But the devil who was a deacon said, "I have led the prelate to get engaged, and now he is planning to marry, because I am his head deacon. He trusts me, and I have my hand in everything. I wrote in his books that bishops are permitted to take a wife." His leader thanked him particularly for this tour de force. Suddenly the cockerel crowed, and the devils jumped from the tree and fled because they are forced to disappear at the first cockcrow.[6]

Lying under the pear tree, the old man had listened to the devils and stayed calm. In the morning, he collected his cockerel and went to the bishop's. He asked to be allowed to enter to give his present, but the deacons refused, explaining that other people had brought finer gifts and had not yet been given permission to enter, while all he had was one little rooster! The old man insisted and remained where he was. The deacons finally told the bishop, who invited the old man to have a seat. "Monsignor, I would like to hear from your own mouth that it's true that you intend to marry."

"That's exactly so."

"How would this be possible, Monsignor? At my age, I've never heard of a bishop getting married, for it is forbidden and contrary to divine law. What's the story now? It's confusing."

"How?" asked the bishop. "It is written in the books that marriage is not forbidden to prelates. Since it isn't a sin, why couldn't I?"

"Monsignor," relied the old man, "you don't know that the devil in person has decreed that bishops are permitted to marry, for your head deacon is a demon."

"How is this possible? He is the most faithful of all and he assists me during mass."

"He's a devil," insisted the old man. "This very night I heard with my own ears how he explained to the other devils what he did to lead you into committing a mortal sin," and he recounted all he had heard.

Anxiously, the prelate added: "How is it possible that he says Mass with me and always behaves in church as if he were in his own home?"

"Have you seen with your own eyes that he remains in the church from the beginning to the end of the Mass?"

"Yes."

"You must have overlooked something. Do you know if he remains in the church during the Elevation, or if he leaves?"

After giving it some thought, the bishop confessed that he did not know. The old man continued: "Since that is the way things are, before celebrating Mass tomorrow morning, have the doors and windows secretly sealed so not even the smallest opening is left. At the time of the Elevation, watch what he does and where he goes."

The bishop followed this advice, and the next morning celebrated Mass with his head deacon, the devil. At the moment of the Elevation, the devil tried to sneak away as he had always done.[7] He raced to the door, then to another, then from window to window. Panicking, he climbed to a window high enough to get out, but couldn't open it. The mass continued and he burst apart and a multitude of mice emerged out of his body. This is how mice first appeared on the Earth and then spread everywhere. Because they are a tribe of the devil, they cause as much harm to humans as devils. Now aware of everything that had happened, the prelate broke his engagement and remained celibate, as required by his position.

AUGUST LESKIEN, *BALKANMÄRCHEN*

(IÉNA: EUGEN DIEDERICHS, 1915), 54–57.

ATU 816.*

The motif that a demon cannot attend a certain part of the Mass is a very ancient one. It can be seen as early as 1217 in the work of Gerald of Wales (De Principium Instructione, *III, 27*), *and in the work of Gervase of Tilbury, whose* Imperial Diversions (Otia Imperialia, *III, 37*) *were written between 1209 and 1214. In Gerald's account, it's an Anjou countess who sneaks away before the host is consecrated; in Gervase's account, it's a chatelaine.*

3. How the Devil Captures a Soul

Finland

An old man who had gone to get wood left his bread on a stump. The devil followed him and ate the bread. "Whoever ate my bread will have to become my servant," said the pauper.

"I'm the one who ate it," said the Prince of Evil.

"Then you must serve me for three years."

"Agreed, but first I'm going to go ask my father for his advice."

His father told him, "Go there and serve him until he becomes rich and dies of drunkenness." He took this advice and told the poor man, "From now on I shall be your servant." But the peasant's wife fumed, "What are we going to do with a servant? We don't even have enough to eat for us and the children!"

The devil then told the peasant, "This year we are going to drain the marsh and grow rye." He cleared the entire marsh, which left very fertile soil where they could sow rye. He then went to get money from his father, and loaned it to the poor man so he could sow the ground. The rye grew so well that there was not enough space in the barn to store all of it.

The next year they wanted to clear another parcel, but the marsh was too wet that year. However, they harvested another huge quantity of rye. "What are we going to do with this harvest?" the devil asked the peasant.

"We'll make whiskey from it and sell it."

They built a distillery and made large amounts of whiskey. At the end of the third year, the man died from too much drink, and his servant carried off his soul. Rejoining his father, he observed: "The poor man behaved so well all his life and the devil could not take any advantage of him, but the rich man who works evil in his lifetime gives us his soul as soon as he dies."

August von Löwis of Menar,
Finnische und estnische Volksmärchen
(Iena: Eugen Diederichs, 1922), 69–70.

📖 Bechstein 13; Schullerus 94.

ATU 810 A.

4. Saint Peter's Wager with the Devil

Austria

Once upon a time two strangers, totally different in appearance, met in a Fischbach tavern. One was a sinister man of uncertain age with black hair and a shifty gaze. The other was a man of a certain age with grey hair and beard, light, malicious eyes, and a reserved attitude. Chance seems to have brought them together, and they sat at the same table. They asked the innkeeper for a refreshing drink and a solid snack. After sharing the reasons for their trip, they realized they had the same objective: visiting the Inn Valley, in particular going to Saint Peter's Mountain, once called the Little Madron.* "It's my mountain," declared the oldest of the two, and he introduced himself to the other as the first of the apostles and saints of Christ. "My name is Peter," he went on to say. "The chapel built on high, the first in the Inn Valley, was dedicated to me. The lands and the people around it belong to the one true God of heaven. Why should it come as a surprise that I would want to go up there to see what the faithful have built for me and how they pay homage to God?"

"That's not at all how it's going to be!" the devil—for that's who the other man was—replied abruptly, "For I will get there before you and destroy all you wish to take possession of with thunderbolts. Nobody will honor you anymore and no one will believe in your God. All will have to obey me!" To put an end to their argument, Saint Peter proposed a wager to the devil: the region would belong to whoever got to the top of the mountain first. With an evil smile, Satan shook Saint Peter's hand to seal the bargain. They paid their tab and set off.

---

*A mountain in the Bavarian Alps.

Saint Peter solemnly scaled the mountainous path while the devil rushed into a rift in the cliff face to make his way to the top. But once he was almost all the way up, a thick slab of rock barred the exit. So close to his objective and so close to getting out, he had to free the passageway at any cost. He finally succeeded in lifting the slab, which weighed tons, only to find himself face-to-face with his opponent, who was already there. Slowly and solemnly, Saint Peter raised his right hand and made the sign of the cross. The Prince of Evil was forced to go back the way he came and dashed into the depths, all the way back to hell. The rift still exists today. Inside it is black and slippery. The locals call it the Devil's Hole.*

MAX EINMAYR, *INNTALER SAGEN, SAGEN UND GESCHICHTEN AUS DEM INNTAL ZWISCHEN KAISERGEBIRGE UND WASSERBURG* (OBERAUDORF: MEISSNER-DRUCK, 1988), S. 92.

5. The Devil's Dance

Poland

When the wind swirls and sends the black sand flying, it's the dance of an evil spirit. If you are scared of the devil, close all your windows then, but if you are brave and ready to sell your soul for wealth and gold, take a sharp new knife, and toss it into the whirlwind.

Once upon a time there was a young peasant whose barn roof had been torn off by the devil in the form of a whirlwind. The lad took a sparkling new knife and threw it into the tornado. The devil appeared at once, humbly bowing. "What is your command?" he asked the young man.

"First of all, repair the barn," yelled the young man, red with

---

*This is an etiological tale attached to the local geography.

rage. "Then fill my potato storehouse with gold. Also bring me a barrel of brandy, fresh bacon, and three large hides."

"So shall it be, but first, pull out the knife that is causing me to suffer horribly."

"No, start by obeying!" And the devil did as he had been ordered. A short time later, the peasant was struck by a disease that brought him to the very gates of death. His neighbors came to visit him and saw, at the head of the patient's bed, the devil lying in wait for his poor soul. They felt full of pity for the poor lad, and his old godmother said softly, "He should not have asked for gold. He would have done better to shoot at the devil with a silver button. He would have gone on to live a long and honest life, and saved his soul."

KASIMIR WLADISLAW WOYCICKI,
POLNISCHE VOLKSSAGEN UND MÄRCHEN
(BERLIN: FRIEDRICH HEINRICH LEWESTAM, 1839), 24–25.

ATU 325.

This legend (it's not a folktale) is based on several beliefs: one is that the devil (or a witch) can take the form of a tornado that can be brought to a stop by stabbing it with a knife. Shooting at a supernatural being with a silver button is a variant of shooting a silver bullet, generally used against werewolves.

6. The Two Butchers in Hell

Transylvania

Once upon a time there were two brothers who were both butchers. One was rich and wicked and the other was poor and kind, but because he could not work for himself, he helped his brother and was paid frugally in kind. One day, when he had practically killed himself performing a task, his brother only gave him one little sausage. "Give me another, I certainly deserve it!"

"Go ahead and take it, and go to the devil!" replied his irritated brother, who threw it at him.

The poor man quietly went back home and slept until morning. He grilled one of the sausages to eat on the road, hanging the other from a staff like gypsies do when bringing meat back from the market. He then headed directly to the devil's house with his staff. But as you can imagine, hell is a long ways away, and he did not get there until the next day. The devils were all out working in the woods and only the grandmother was there, looking out the window. The butcher greeted her politely. "Good day, grandmother, how are you?"

"Fine, my son, but what brings you here? Usually no man comes here of his free will."

"I would not have come if my brother had not sent me here with this sausage," he said, handing it to her with his staff. The grandmother caught it through the window, thanked him, and invited him in. "Gladly," said the poor man, "I'm going to be able to warm myself at your fire, and reheat my sausage, because it is devilishly cold outside." The grandmother did everything to make things pleasant for him, and when evening fell she hid him under her bed so that the devils who would come back starving would not find him. They soon appeared and shouted: "Something to eat, something to eat. Hunger is such torture. Ah, that smells like human flesh, no?" They walked around the room sniffing, but the grandmother calmed them by placing a steaming pot of stew on the table. "There was a man here," she told them, "but he fled; that's why you can smell him." They were satisfied with this explanation and after eating threw themselves in their beds, slept until morning, and then went back to the woods.

The grandmother then told the butcher he could come out from beneath the bed and said, "You can now peacefully return

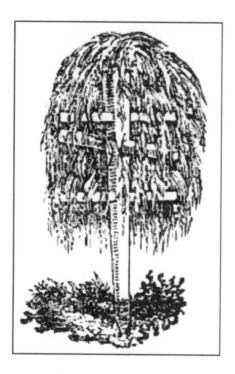

Hay Pole

home." Then she snatched a hair that had fallen from one of the devils overnight from a pillow, and gave it to her guest with these words: "Once you are back home, you will see what treasure is there." The butcher thanked her for her friendly hospitality and for the gift, and then ended with a polite, "May God bless you, grandmother!" before leaving.

Once he reached his home, the hair grew to the size of a hay pole* made of pure gold.

The poor brother, who was now wealthier than his brother, could now work on his own behalf, and hired several journeymen. Extremely jealous, his brother couldn't stand being less rich than his own brother. Having learned how his brother had gotten rich, one day he took a large fat sausage and made his way to hell. Once there, he spotted the grandmother at the window. "What are you

---

*Cf. illustration. In France this framework is called a grass parrot.

doing there, you old witch?" he shouted meanly, without even saying hello.

"I'm waiting for your sausage."

"It's certainly not you who's going to get her teeth into it! I am bringing it for the devils in exchange for a gold hay pole."

"Very well. Enter and wait here for the devils to come home from the woods in the evening." The butcher entered and sat on a chair behind the door. When the famished devils returned, they were all bellowing with hunger. Soon after, they smelled the stranger and started yelling: "That smells like human flesh!"

"The roast is behind the door," their grandmother told them. They hurled themselves on the butcher and ripped him to pieces.

His brother inherited everything his stingy, greedy brother had owned. So goes the way of the world, if only it were ever thus!

JOSEF HALTRICH, DEUTSCHE VOLKSMÄRCHEN AUS DEM SACHSENLANDE IN SIEBENBÜRGEN (VIENNA: VERLAG VON CARL GRAESER, JULIUS SPRINGER, 1856), 170–172.

7. The Devil and the Three Young Slavs

Hungary

Once upon a time in Slavonia there was a man with three sons. On fine day he told them: "My children, go out and discover the world. There is a land where the chipping sparrow bathes in wine and the fences are made of grilled sausages,* and if you want luck to smile on your undertakings, start by learning the language of this land."

---

*An allusion to the Land of Cockaigne.

This description enchanted the three brothers, who were possessed by a keen desire to visit this country. Their father accompanied them to a mountain three days walk away, and once at the top they had reached the frontier of this blessed land. Their father gave them an empty knapsack, and showing the eldest son what direction to go in, and exclaimed, "Can't you see Hungary?" He then took leave of his sons, convinced that he had given them the key to happiness.

Once on their own, they made their way into Hungary, and resolved to learn the local language in accordance with their father's command. After crossing the border, they met a man who asked them where they were going and what they intended to do. "Learn Hungarian," they answered.

"My children, don't go any farther," said the man. "With me you will learn it in three days instead of an entire year."

The three young men accepted his proposal and, on the third day, he had taught the first one to say "we three," the second, "for a cheese," and the third "it's like that." Satisfied with this lesson, the young Slavs didn't wish to learn anything else and resumed their journey.

They soon came to a forest, where they stumbled upon a murdered man in the middle of the path. They examined him and with fright realized it was the man they had just left. While they were sighing in sorrow and dismay, a sergeant appeared to interrogate them. "Who killed this man?" The first boy answered "We three," because he didn't know how to say anything else.

"Why?" asked the sergeant.

"For a cheese," replied the second.

"If that's the case," the policeman went on, "then you will be hanged."

"That's how it is," replied the third.

The three lads were taken away to be hanged. In the meantime, the dead man got back up, shook himself, and reassumed his true appearance: first a donkey, then a wolf, and finally that of a red-headed devil,* whose mocking laughter followed the three young Slavs whose stupidity had landed them in his snare.

GEORG STIER, UNGARISCHE SAGEN UND MÄRCHEN
(BERLIN: FERDINAND DÜMMLER, 1850), 25–28.

8. Happy Are Those Who Place Their Faith in the Devil

Albania

Once upon a time there was a man who lit candles for the saints without anything coming of it. He then contemplated lighting one for the devil, bought a candle, and lit it. That evening he prayed to the Prince of Evil for his aid. The devil appeared to him in a dream and said, "You who did me the honor of lighting a candle for me, I will make you a present of four acres of land," which brought comfort to our hero. "I'm now rich!" he said jubilantly.

"Wait a moment, you must set your boundary markers," the devil said.

They looked here, they looked there, always with the same result—nothing. "It doesn't matter," said the Evil One. "Marking the field's borders is not hard, you only have to make water at its four corners and place the boundary markers later."

"Right away!" Still dreaming, the man got up, urinated on the four corners of his mattress, then lay down again. When he got up the next morning he saw to his surprise that he had wet the bed and asked himself, "Am I awake or still asleep?" He turned around to look at his mattress, saw he wasn't sleeping and said to

---

*The structure of the phrase suggests these forms follow each other.

himself: "Happy is he who places his hope in the devil, for he will get favors!"

Johann Georg von Hahn, <i>Griechische und
albanesische Märchen</i>, 1. Teil
(Leipzig: Wilhelm Engelmann, 1864).

9. The Devil's Payment

Romania

Once upon a time there was a woman whose husband was a shepherd. He was not often home, which his wife found unpleasant because she felt lonely without him. Time passed. Not only did she get used to his absences, but ended up feeling that he came back home too often, which distracted her from her chats with the Orthodox priest who had come to ease her solitude until she started liking him better than her husband. When her spouse left to keep watch over the sheep, she got brandy and cooked waffles, and the priest would come over to eat and drink with her. When it was time for her husband to come home, the priest would slip away. A time came when they ardently wished the husband would disappear, and they put their heads together to figure out the best way to get rid of him. The woman had an idea that she immediately put to work: when she heard her husband returning, she lay down and welcomed him with dreadful moans. "I'm sick, I'm going to die, only Danube water can save me. Go to the banks of that river, dear husband, and bring me back some of this water so I can rub it on my back. Maybe it will heal me."

The husband put on his *houpplande* [greatcoat], took a pitcher, and then walked and walked until he reached the Danube. The devil was standing on its bank in the shape of an old man. "Where are you going?" he asked.

"That's none of your concern," the shepherd replied brusquely.

"Tell me the truth! Where are you going and what do you want? You can't get rid of me so easily!"

Realizing he was not dealing with an ordinary man, the shepherd told him how his wife was very ill and had asked him for Danube water with which to rub her back.

"Fine, what will you give me if I quickly transport you back home so you can see what your wife is up to while you are gone to fetch the water?"

"Whatever you want."

"Because you told me the truth, I'm going to take you home immediately and I will get my reward. Slip into this sack. With my sack on my back, and my violin under the *bubau*,* I'm going to visit your village as if I were a peddler."

Once the man was in his sack, the devil hoisted it over his back and in the blink of an eye was by the door of the shepherd's house. Through the window, they could see the priest sitting at a table laden with waffles and brandy. The devil rapped at the window, and said in a plaintive voice, "Good folk, let me in, your house is the only one that is not dark for the night. I would be satisfied with a little place by the stove or behind the door." The priest and the woman decided to let him come in, as there was plenty of room. The devil entered and set the sack down behind the door. "What have you got under your coat?' the wife asked.

"A violin."

Play us a tune so we can dance!"

The devil did not wait to be asked twice, but pulled out his instrument and began to play and sing:

*This word of Hungarian origin describes a long-haired peasant coat. We would like to thank Emanuela Timotin, who provided us this information.

Tralala, Tralali, Tralala
Just you wait a little
Soon the devil will be laughing at you

Snapping his tongue, the priest spun the wife around while she sang:

I had a kind husband
I sent him to fetch me Danube water
To caress my back with
Hi Hi Hi.

Aiee, aiee, aiee, the song changed into howls and tears because her husband, leaping out of the sack, started caressing her back, not with Danube water but with a solid stick to heal her of her fondness for the priest who, for his part, jumped out of the window in front of the devil, who laughed himself out of breath—that was his payment!

Pauline Schullerus, *Rumänische Volksmärchen aus dem mittleren Harbachtal* (Bukarest: Kriterion, 1977), 388–90.

ATU 1360 C, EM 6, 1011–1017.

CHAPTER VII

SINGULAR TALES

1. The Devil's Boat

Karelia, Finland

One day a hunter took his crossbow and headed into the forest. He ended up coming upon a place where the heirs to a dead man had gathered. They had much treasure, such as golden plates and spoons, and each had a gold vehicle. They were all joint owners of a golden boat that moved on its own volition as soon as someone climbed on board. When the devils spotted the hunter and his crossbow, they called out to him: "Come, my fine fellow, and share this wealth with us. You will be rewarded!" He approached and asked, "How do you work these vehicles and this boat?"

"If you climb to the highest yardarm while having your feet on the lowest one," they replied, "the vehicles and boat* will move on their own."

He then pointed his crossbow, shot an arrow from it, and told them: "Go fetch the arrow I just shot. The first one to get it will obtain a vehicle and the gold boat." The devils raced off in search of the arrow and ran so far they could neither be seen nor heard.

---

*We have to think that the vehicles are accessories of the boat.

Realizing they were a long ways away, the hunter said to himself, "They're going to be back in a hurry." He quickly filled the boat with all the vehicles and treasure, and jumped aboard. He climbed to the highest yardarm and placed his feet on the lower one. The ship set off, crossing many lands and seas[1] until it came to a stop in front of a king's castle. The monarch's daughter was sitting on the staircase. Seeing the golden ship approaching, she waved to the hunter and said, "He must be the most powerful emperor of the world who travels on this boat. If you bring me with you, dear emperor, I will marry you."

"Princess," he replied, "I'm only a farmhand not even worthy of shining your shoes. There are more than enough kings for you to choose from." But even though she realized he was only a peasant, she insisted and said, "Let me come on board. I want to marry you."

"You're making fun of me," he replied. "There are plenty of kings around." In the end, she brought him all sorts of drinks and fine foods as well as clothing, hats, and boots, but they remained in a pile on the bridge because the hunter did not even dare touch them. During this time, the princess paced and paced, buried in her sad and bitter thoughts, because he scorned her.

The hunter thought on the matter for a week, and noting that the princess was not joking, he told her, "Most dear princess, if you truly wish to marry a farmhand, come aboard!" She did just that. He kneeled and asked her, "Where are we going now, dear princess?"

"Let's sail over the vast sea," she replied. "There is an island there that is ten leagues long. Countless berries grow there and fruits carpet the ground."

The hunter set sail and the boat came to the middle of an island and stopped. The man left the boat to fetch berries, but barely had he tasted one when he fell into a deep slumber. He began to snore, and when she realized that he was not coming back with anything for her, the princess lost her temper and screamed: "Die on this island, then, wretched farmhand! I'm turning around and going back home." She did exactly this, while the hunter remained behind sleeping.

When he finally emerged from his slumber, there was no sign of the boat or the treasures belonging to the devils. All he had left was a little purse with silver. He was as hungry as a wolf and had nothing to eat. He approached a bush covered with berries, with which he filled his left pocket. He put one in his mouth, bit it, and swallowed. But they were cursed, and monstrous horns grew out of his head.[2] They were so heavy his neck could hardly hold them up. He was flooded with fear. "I could handle all this," he thought to himself, "although I'm dreadfully famished, if I only didn't have these horns. If any sailors land here, they will mistake me for a wild beast and kill me!" While bemoaning his fate, he passed near another bush, stopped, and filled his right pocket with its fruits. He ate a berry, but this time they were beneficial, and after he swallowed it his horns fell off, leaving no trace on his head.[3] The hunter's beauty was enhanced so much that none could match it in the kingdom.

He waited on the island for a boat whose route would carry it past there, and when he finally spotted a sail, he shouted, "Come get me, my friends, I beg you, rescue me from this island! Let me sail with you, and then show me the way to the royal palace, from where I left with my boat." They accepted and set him down on dry land, telling him which direction to travel to reach the castle.

The hunter entered the courtyard of the royal residence, where he found a fountain with a spout equipped with a faucet. He sat down on the edge, plunged his dirty feet in the water, and began to shake them, dirtying the water. The monarch's head chef spotted him from atop the castle's staircase. If he had been malicious, he would have shouted out at once: "Why have you dirtied our fountain? It would be annoying for us, but worse for the king and his wife!" The king would have then heard him and ordered the hunter's head to be cut off. But the cook, a kind and gentle man, approached the hunter and said, "Oh, poor wretch, you have gotten the water of our fountain dirty! It will be really annoying for us to drink this water, but much worse for the king and their Royal Highnesses! If the monarch learns of this, he will have your head."

"Dear friend, don't tell anyone," begged the hunter. "I will give you the means to become as handsome as me."

"Fine, if you tell me how to do that, I will keep my mouth shut," the cook replied.

Immediately the hunter gave him several berries to eat. Once he had eaten and swallowed them, his beauty was equal to that of the hunter, who went and hid. In the meantime, the master chef had prepared the king's lunch. They ate, drank, and laughed all through the meal. After lunch, the princess went to see the cook and asked him: "How did you suddenly become so handsome?"

"There is a stranger in the courtyard who knows how to enhance the beauty of any who wishes it."

The princess, the same one who had taken the boat, said, "If he makes me more beautiful, I will marry him."

"He has to have left; he feared being killed in this foreign city," the cook replied.

"Tell him there is no reason in the world for him to be scared, for I will protect him. If he comes to the castle, I will treat him well."

The hunter arrived and was led into a side room. The princess brought him all he needed to feast well. While he was restoring himself, she sat down near him and said, "Brave man, make me as beautiful as the cook and I will marry you." But he resented her for having left him on the island, and while continuing to eat and drink, he replied, "Friendly princess, I, a simple farmhand, am not worthy of marrying you; there are kings for that."

"If there are no other ways to gain your trust," replied the princess, who did not recognize the man she had abandoned, "I will give you a general's uniform, as well as gold and golden cups. Moreover, I own a golden boat and gold vehicles that I will also give you." The hunter thought, "In any case, they are already mine," but he said nothing. The princess persisted, "I won't leave you alone until you grant me my wish." The man accepted, but the rascal took the berries from his left pocket to give her, and then hid. As soon as the princess had eaten a few berries, two enormous horns sprouted from her head. The king wanted them sawed off, but in vain. Two strong soldiers were ordered to hold her bent over backwards so the young maiden could move. Finally, the king had it proclaimed throughout the kingdom that if a bachelor could heal his daughter and remove her horns, he would marry her and be made a general. If a married man or woman was responsible for healing her, he or she would be given enough wealth to last until the end of their days.

The royal palace became crowded with doctors trying to heal the maiden, but all their treatments were useless. In the end, the hunter stepped out of the crowd, knelt before the king, and said to him: "Your grace, let me try to heal the princess and free her from her horns."

"My poor boy," the monarch replied, "do you think you have the power to do that? Everyone there has already tried their best, but their only success has been to eat and drink as if there were no tomorrow."

"Sire, those folk are incapable of breaking the horns. I alone have the power to do so."

"Try, my dear son. I will name you general as soon as the horns fall off my daughter's head."

"Send all these charlatans packing and have your soldiers proclaim throughout the kingdom the good news: I am going to heal your daughter."

All the quacks were immediately driven away, and the soldiers marched off to announce the good news. The hunter remained with the young woman and some servants who had come in to help him. He ordered one of these servants: "Light the stove in the sauna and heat the bath." To the valet, he said: "Bring me back from the forest three thin willow wands, then soften them in water. I can use them to banish the horns."

All well and good, once the wands were softened and the sauna was heated with hot water, the hunter led the maiden inside, sent the servants away, and locked the door. During this time, the army outside was shouting joyfully. The hunter grabbed the princess, hung her by her horns, and began to whip her, saying, "Will you leave me again to die at sea? Will you flee again with all I own? I am your fiancé now and you cannot make fun of me anymore." She begged him: "Stop hitting me! I'll never do you wrong again!" He gave her a berry from his right pocket and her horns fell, leaving no trace. The princess became so beautiful that there were none in the kingdom as beautiful as the two of them. The jubilation at the castle was great: people ate, drank, and danced, and the hunter was named a general and married the princess. That's how the story ends.

EMMY SCHRECK, *FINNISCHE MÄRCHEN*
(WEIMAR: HERMANN BÖHLAU, 1887), 27–35.

ANTTI AARNE, "DIE DREI ZAUBERGEGENSTÄNDE UND
DIE WUNDERBAREN FRÜCHTE," IN A. AARNE *VERGLEICHENDE
MÄR- CHENFORSCHUNGEN* (HELSINFORS:
FINNO-UGRIAN SOCIETY, 1908), 83–142.

📖 Obert 8 ; Papahagi, *Basme aromâne*, n° 21; Pauline Schullerus, *Rumänische Volks- märchen aus dem Harbachtal,* n° 87.

ATU 566, BP I, 464-485, EM V, 7-14, MLEX 755–748.

This tale appears to be a variant of the story of Fortunatus, but instead of inheriting or receiving magical objects, our hero steals

them from devils, whose sole role is to explain their origin. The
owners vary depending on the country.

2. The Carpenter, Perkūnas, and the Devil

Lithuania

Once he finished learning a trade as a carpenter, a young man had a yen to see the country. After he had been traveling for several days, he met a man following the same route, and they decided to travel together in order for time to pass by more quickly while walking. As they traveled, he learned that his companion was Perkūnas.* The next day, they met a man who told them he was the devil. The three traveled together and made their way into a vast forest where many wild animals lived. Because they had nothing to eat, the devil said, "I am strong and quick; I am going to bring us back meat, bread, and whatever else we need."

"I am going to start thundering and throwing lightning bolts," said Perkūnas, "so once the fires my bolts kindle everywhere are raging, the wild animals will come fleeing right into our hands."

And the carpenter added, "I will bake and cook everything you bring back." In accordance with this agreement, everyone did what he had promised, and they lived in the wild for several weeks this way.

After some time had passed, the carpenter said, "Listen, comrades! Let's build a beautiful house in which we will be able to live like all men. Why continue living so frugally like savages?" The suggestion appealed to his two companions. All the carpenter

---

*Perkūnas is the god of lightning in Lithuanian mythology. The Prussians called him Perkons; in Russia his name is Perun.

had to do was find the trees he wanted, and the other two would immediately tear them out by the roots and drag them to where he wanted to build. When they thought they had enough wood, they began construction. It was the carpenter's job to do the measurements and draw, it was up to the other two to remove the branches and bark from the trees, and in a very short time there stood a pretty little house. They settled in quite comfortably, as the carpenter only needed to explain what needed to be done and how for the other two to execute it immediately. They then made a field in the clearing. The carpenter built a plow to which he hitched his two companions, and they began clearing away all the stumps, roots, and stones without any problem. He then built an enormous harrow and used it on the field with his two companions. In several days they had a beautiful plot of arable land. With the ground now ready, the devil provided all kinds of vegetable seeds, which they sowed and planted, especially turnips.

When the vegetables and turnips had grown quite a bit, they discovered that they were being robbed, but had no idea who the criminal was.[4] They made a plan to keep watch at night. On the first night it was the devil's turn. While he was standing watch, the robber arrived and began loading the vegetables into a cart. The devil leapt up to punch him, but the thief battered him so mercilessly that he barely kept his life, after which he fled with the turnips. In the morning the carpenter came with Perkūnas to see how things were, but they found that the devil was moaning of his many injuries, and that a lot of vegetables were gone. The devil told them, "Last night, I didn't feel very well, and once I started feeling better I fell asleep, and that's when the robber struck."

The next night, Perkūnas stood guard, but the same misfortune befell him. When he tried to grab the criminal, the thief gave him a serious thrashing and left with a cart full of turnips. The next morning, his companions saw the damage, and when the carpenter scolded Perkūnas about it, he replied: "Last night, I had a terrible toothache, and once it calmed down I fell asleep, which is when the thief carried off the turnips." Neither he nor the devil wished to admit they had been beaten up so badly.

On the third night, it was the carpenter's turn to stand watch. As he was also an amateur musician, he took his violin, sat beneath a spruce tree and when he felt sleepy, kept himself awake by playing, because he wanted to remain totally alert to identify the thief. Around midnight, he heard the thief heading directly to the turnip field, cracking his whip while saying: "Crack! Iron cart, crack! Little whip with metal strips!" and so on. The thoughts in the carpenter's head were jostling each other as he redoubled his violin playing. When the thief heard the music he stopped and became quiet. The carpenter redoubled his efforts, again hoping to scare away the thief that way, but was unsuccessful. The robber liked the music and he came closer. Who was it? A wild and alarming Laume* who lived in the forest and whom none could defeat. This was the being responsible for stealing the turnips and beating up the devil and Perkūnas. Knowing what had happened to his companions, the carpenter believed that caution was called for. The creature approached him, wishing him a good evening and being quite friendly, because it greatly liked the music. After listening for a moment, the creature said to him, "Be kind enough to let me try." But it could not entice any sound out of the instrument. The carpenter took it by the hand and showed it how to do it, but with no result despite its strong desire to learn. The woodland creature said, "I would be extremely grateful to you if you taught me how to play."

"It's a trifle for me," he replied. "I know what you must do; follow my advice and you will be able to play without any delay."

"I will do whatever you say," it replied.

---

*The Laume is sometimes a fairy and sometimes a woodland spirit.

"Look how big your fingers are, and then look at mine! You must make yours smaller in order to play."

The Laume accepted. The carpenter went to get his axe and a wedge, looked around for an enormous stump, split it, and stuck the wedge in until the rent was large enough for the Laume to slip its fingers inside. Once the fingers of both hands were in the crack, he pulled out the wedge. The crack snapped shut,[5] crushing the thief's fingers so hard that blood began to flow. The creature howled in pain and begged the carpenter to free it, promising to never again steal their turnips.[6] He left it trapped while he went to fetch its whip with the iron strips, and began to hit it. When he felt the punishment was sufficient, he used the wedge to open the crack, which allowed the Laume to free its fingers. It fled like the wind, abandoning its little cart and its whip.

Early that morning, they could all see that not a single turnip had gone missing. The carpenter made fun of the other two, telling them: "Here are a pair of good-for-nothings! You act all boastful when a poor old lady gave you a complete thrashing. But I paid her back so well that she will never still our turnips again." His two companions began to fear him, imagining that he was particularly strong. Until then they had thought that, compared to them, he was a weakling, but now they held him in high esteem and no longer felt any need to guard the garden. The Laume never returned to steal again.

Several years later, they decided it was time to part; it would be better for one of them to remain there but they couldn't agree on which one would get to keep the house. Indeed, each thought they were responsible for the lion's share of its construction. After many long arguments, this is what they decided: night after night, each of them would take turns trying to scare the others,[7] and the house would belong to the one who best resisted fear and was most successful at forcing the other two companions to flee. The first night, the devil tried his luck. At midnight, a very powerful wind rose up and an enormous racket shook the house, which began creaking and cracking. The ceilings moved and the timber beams shifted. Perkūnas then rushed out the window,[8] but the carpenter took his hymn book and sang and prayed without moving a muscle, despite all the commotion and storms caused by the devil, who sounded as if he were trying to tear the house off its foundations, shake it, and turn it upside down. Perkūnas had lost the wager and the carpenter had won.

The next night, Perkūnas went out to scare them, and the devil and the carpenter remained in the main room. When the night was already well advanced, a cloud black as pitch appeared, producing terrible thunder and lightning flashes. The closer the cloud got to the house, the more violent the thunder and lightning became. It was easy to believe that the entire forest and the house were going to be swallowed up in the very depths of the Earth. The flashes and explosions had become so intense that everything seemed poised to catch on fire.

When he saw this, quick as a flash, the devil leaped through the window and fled, because he didn't trust Perkūnas and feared he would kill him with a lightning bolt. He knew full well that Perkūnas killed the devils that hung around the world. Grabbing his book, the carpenter sang and prayed, sparing no thought for the horrors of Perkūnas. Again he won the wager, while the devil lost his.

On the third night, the carpenter went out to scare the other two. Perkūnas and the devil remained inside and thought: "How could he terrorize us?" But around eleven o'clock, our hero went to fetch the Laume's iron cart and his whip with the metal strips, which he had hidden in some bushes in the forest without breathing a word of it. He thought, "If I go back to the house in this device, they will be scared." He got in the cart and began cracking the whip. The cart began racing toward the house while he shouted, "Crack, iron cart, crack, little whip with the metal strips!"

When they heard this, the other two imagined it was the Laume, the same one who had given both of them quite a thrashing earlier. They became so panic-stricken, they were not able to resist for long. Perkūnas fled through the window, spitting fire all around him, while the devil got diarrhea and, after soiling himself, went out through the roof. Neither of them were ever seen again. This was how the carpenter became sole proprietor of such a prettily designed house. He cleaned up the devil's soiling and brought it to the apothecary, where he sold it for a pretty penny. For many years he lived in ease and happiness, until the day he died. And, even today, apothecaries sell the devil's droppings as a remedy.*

AUGUST SCHLEICHER, *LITAUISCHE MÄRCHEN, SPIRCHWORTE, RÄTSEL UND LIEDER* (WEIMAR: BÖHLAU, 1857), 145 *FF.*

3. How the Devil Abducted a Fisherman's Son

Lithuania

Once upon a time there was a fisherman who wrote on a piece of paper: "I live free of cares." He signed it and nailed it to a stake bordering the road that the king used for his strolls, and this is how the king spotted the piece of paper and read it. He exclaimed: "Here I am king and I have worries, and a simple sinner doesn't have a single one!" He ordered the man to catch a fish with diamonds for eyes and gold scales in three days. Indeed, three days later a great reception would be given at court, and the monarch wanted to serve a fish the likes of which no king had ever seen. It's then that the fisherman became anxious. He fished all day and all night and only caught the usual kinds of fish! The second day

---

*The text plays with the two meanings of *teufesldreck:* "shit of the devil," and "asafoetida," a plant with a strong smell of sulfur.

he started over and prayed to God before casting his net, but still only caught the regular fish. On the third day, on his way to go fishing, he asked the devil for help. In the blink of an eye, the demon was by his side, saying, "Promise to let me have something that is not yet at your house, and I will help you." The fisherman thought about it and believed he had left at home everything he owned so he replied: "Understood, I promise it to you."

"In twenty years, on this day of this month, I will come to fetch what's owed me," replied the devil, who disappeared.

The fisherman cast his net and pulled from the water a fish like the one described by the king. Great was the stupefaction at court when he brought it to the king, who told him: "You have lived without cares; henceforth, you shall have even fewer."

The fisherman returned home, where, in the meantime, his wife had given birth to a son. Remembering his promise to the devil,[9] he felt fear, but spoke of it to no one, not even his wife. The child grew, and at three years old he was a handsome little lad. One day when the king was going by, he caught sight of the child and went to find the fisherman. "I have no son, I'm going to take yours with me,"[10] the king told him. The monarch gave him a good education and considered him as his own child.

The day arrived when the devil came to claim his prey. The lad was out walking and the fisherman, who had left the house in tears, ran into him. "Why are you crying, Father?"

"I won't tell you."

"If you don't answer me," the young man replied, "I'll have your head cut off!"

His father then told him how he had once promised him to the devil, and that the Prince of Evil would come to fetch him that very night. The lad returned to the castle and told the story to the sovereign, who had sentinels posted at all the doors and windows.

But in the morning, the king found his guards dead. The following night he doubled the sentinels, but again found all of them dead the next day. The fisherman's son then told him, "It's unfortunate that you have sacrificed so many soldiers. I will spend the next night outdoors." That evening, he set up in the courtyard with a small table and a chair. Then, with his knife, he drew a circle around him as far as his hand could reach, placed a candle on the table, and took out his book of hours, with the intention of praying all night. When night fell, six devils appeared before him, saying: "Come now, we have waited for you long enough!" Without even glancing at them, he continued to pray. After the demons had waited a few moments, they were joined by nine more devils. They barraged him with questions, but he ignored them. At the stroke of midnight, they approached with the noise of a tempest and pulled the table and the young man out of the circle.* One of them grabbed him and carried him off in the air.

The fisherman's son then remembered that his book contained a pious image depicting Christ's crucifixion. He turned to the devil, showing him the image. "I can't stand the sight of that," screamed the demon.

"Then put me down on the ground!" he replied, but was met with a solid refusal. The lad then showed him another image that was even more intolerable, and the devil shouted, "Get that away from me!"

"Then put me down!" Loosening his hold, the devil let him fall.

As he fell he thought he would land on the ground, but he fell into the chimney of an enchanted castle. He crawled inside as far as his hips, then, twisting and turning, let himself slip through it to the ground. He found himself in a dark room, but was able to find the door and make his way into a second room, where a light was shining. He sat down and prayed. Then three maidens came in who were black as coal. They asked him, "How did you get here?" He explained what had happened and they told him:

---

*This is surprising as the circle should have protected him. The boy likely forgot to inscribe holy names or to draw a cross inside it.

"If you can stand being mistreated for three nights in a row, your happiness is guaranteed and we will be free.[11] But if you can't put up with it to the bitter end, that will be the end of all of us." The fisherman's son agreed, and that evening they put him into bed in the room where they normally slept, and went off to hide.

Three devils then popped in and spent the night tossing him from one bed to another, without him making the slightest cry. In the morning when he rose, a ray of light came through the chimney and he saw that the faces of the three maidens were now white.[12] "Hold firm for two more nights," they implored him, "and this castle will come out of the ground."

The following night there were even more devils, and they treated him so brutally that by morning he was half dead. The ray of light now came through the top halves of the windows, and the young maidens were white from the waist up. "Resist one more night, but it will be worse than the first two," they urged him.

On the third evening, nine demons spent the night tossing him around on twelve beds, and at cockcrow they tore him to pieces and vanished.[13] Now the castle was entirely out of the ground. The three maidens gathered the pieces of the lad's body, put them back together, and restored him to life.[14] He jumped up, exclaiming, "What a good night's sleep I got!"

"You slept so well that your blood splattered the entire bedroom!" they replied. "Now you get to choose which of the three of us you prefer; she will be your wife and you shall rule over the kingdom."

"If I choose the youngest one, the two oldest won't hold it against me?"

"Absolutely not!" So he married the youngest maiden.

He would have liked to know what was going on in his own country, but his wife explained to him that it was very far away, that this was the seventh kingdom.* She gave him a ring that he

---

*This is a sibylline way to express a remote distance.

only needed to twist for it to take him wherever he wanted to go.[15] In an instant, he was back in his homeland, where numerous kings had gathered at his adoptive father's place. They were wondering how the young man might have died, and were very grieved at the thought. He entered and told them, "Don't cry, I'm alive!" Joy was widespread and the king organized a large party. The young man told how he was married, but no one believed him. "If you want, my wife can be here in the blink of an eye," he replied. He went out, then twisted his ring on his finger while thinking: "If only my wife were here." She then appeared. But she had no wish to linger and wanted to return to her kingdom with him, while he wanted to remain a guest of the monarch. While they were getting some fresh air, he fell asleep. She took her ring back from him, woke him up, and said, "Farewell! I will wait for you for seven years. If you haven't returned from here by then, I will marry someone else."[16] Then she vanished. He then realized he did not have the ring anymore, and sadly returned to the king's palace.

The seventh year was almost up and the young king had still not arrived. He was traveling through an immense forest and had come to a hermit's[17] house at dusk. He asked him, "Do you know if I'm still far from my home?"

"You have yet forty leagues to cross," the hermit replied, "and your wife is going to remarry tomorrow."

He spied a coat and hat hanging on the wall, and beneath them a pair of boots. "Tell me, old man, what do you use those boots for?" he asked.

"When I slip them on, I can go forty leagues in a single stride."[18]

"And the hat?"

"When I turn it, I find myself wherever I wish to be in a mere instant."[19]

"And the coat?"

"When I put it on, I become invisible."[20]

The young king waited for the hermit to fall asleep, then he put on the boots and hat and wrapped himself in the coat and left the hermitage.

He took one step and found himself at his wife's home, where preparations were underway to celebrate the wedding. He strolled around without being seen. The fiancé then rolled up in a coach, and when he got out of the vehicle, the young sovereign tripped him so he fell. The fiancé tried to make his way to the balcony where his future bride was standing, but again he fell. When he tried to kiss his fiancée, he fell for a third time. Seeing this, the young woman said, weeping, "I have waited seven years for my husband. I will wait another seven years and not marry anyone else." At that moment, the king took off his coat and his return was celebrated, as was right and proper.

AUGUST LESKIEN & K. BRUGMAN, *LITAUISCHE VOLKSLIEDER UND MÄRCHEN* (STRASBOURG: TRÜBNER, 1882), 410–412.

ATU 756 B + 435 (IN PART).

Several clues suggest that the wife of the fisherman's son is a supernatural being, most likely a fairy captured with her sisters by a demon: her place of residence, the way people get there, and her possession of a magic ring.

4. The Child Promised to the Devil

Germany

In a small street of Clausthal* there long lived a woman who had promised her son to the devil in hopes that he would bring her great advantages. When the time came for the devil to come and

---

*In the Harz (Lower Saxony).

fetch her child, she went away, leaving her son in the house. That evening, at sunset, the boy was sitting at a table and the women were spinning. Not a noise could be heard except the purr of the spinning wheel and the breath of the wind. It was a horrible evening. Suddenly a loud tapping could be heard in the chimney and then in the wood stove, so awful it caused the women to lose their sight and hearing. They couldn't get out; the door was jammed, but they had to escape. They hopped over to a window, screaming for the lad to follow them. "I can't move from where I am," he yelled. "It's like I'm stuck here." Leaving him there, they raced to the neighbors as quick as they could to get help. When they returned, the boy was no longer in his place, the walls were splattered with blood, and the entire room was destroyed. Everything was upside down, tables and benches all overturned. In the middle of the room lay the child, his arms and legs crushed, dead.

AUGUST EY, *HARZMÄRCHENBUCH*
(STADE: F. STREUDEL, 1862), 18 FF.

5. The Son of the Bewitched Count

Tyrol, Austria

Once upon a time there was a very wealthy count who owned many fields and forests, as well as many castles and tenant farms. Countless treasures were heaped up in his keep, and the old saying that the appetite grows with eating certainly applied to this nobleman. Not far away lived another count who also owned large properties, and whose wealth was equal to that of the first. That he was not the only one to rule like a prince over the entire region gnawed away at the greedy and proud count's heart. He thought day and night of ways he could eliminate his rival so he could take possession of his holdings. It was hard, because the noble count was beloved and powerful, and he certainly would have carried the day in any open battle. The miser only wanted to take action if the result was guaranteed. What to do? He shut himself away to hatch dark designs, but none were to his liking. He therefore went into the forest where a wizard lived, to question him.

He leapt onto his steed, spurred him on at top speed, and traveled deep into the darkened woods to visit the magician.* For a large sum of money, the wizard gave him a lock pick plant for opening gates and doors and a magic wand.[21] Whomever was struck by this wand would be changed into a horse. After the count had received these objects and been instructed in how to use them, he returned to his castle feeling quite satisfied. He armed his loyal followers, and during one dark night silently made his way to his rival's dwelling. He opened the door with the plant, and the watchman was killed before he could react. They did the same to all the servitors. The miser made his way into the bedroom and stabbed the noble count[22] with a dagger. As for his only son, who was asleep in his bed, he touched him with his magic wand and the child was instantly changed into a white horse.[23] The murderer entrusted the task of guarding the castle and the horse to two faithful servitors, and returned home with the rest of his host as if nothing had happened. Their return trip was made in complete silence and no one in the land had any suspicion about the nocturnal crime. The sight of his desires fulfilled gave the count much cause to rejoice, for his heart was cold and hard as stone, and his conscience had abandoned him long ago.

But the next day, while his two servitors were sitting in the paneled room of the squires, a hellish noise echoed throughout the vanquished castle. The horses began neighing in the courtyard and in the stalls, and horsemen with clinking spurs appeared to be climbing and descending the staircases.[24] Doors began open-

_____

*The text uses "wizard" and "magician" interchangeably.

ing and shutting without stop, the windows began jingling, and
even the benches and chairs began to move.[25] The two servitors,
who had courageously faced death in many battles, began trembling like leaves and hid in a corner. But the din only grew louder
and, finally, the murdered valets and squires entered the room,[26]
sat at the table, and terrorized the two guards until daybreak. The
hauntings then ended and a deathly silence ruled over the entire
castle. The next evening, the racket resumed, even louder, and
the two servitors decided death was preferable to living through
another night of terror. They fed the horses, locked all the doors
and the gate, then returned to the castle where they told the count
what they had experienced. "We won't spend another night, at any
price, in that haunted castle," they told him. The count mocked
them for their cowardice and sent two new guards, with the same
result. The very next day they also said they planned to leave this
alarming house. Forewarned by this, the other servitors felt no
desire to attempt this venture, and remained deaf to their master's
pleas despite his most tantalizing promises.

The count then summoned his old valet and told him,
"Martin, you have never lacked for courage, and you have always
ignored fear. If you agree to guard the castle, I will treat you as
if you were my very own son. Every day you will have whatever
you want to eat and drink, and I will reward you royally for your
services." Hesitant, the man scratched his ear, but as the count
continued insisting, he yielded and made his way to the lugubri-
ous castle, after getting orders to never give the horse more than a
handful of hay a day.

So the old valet ended up living by himself at the castle.
He slept during the day because the commotion at night was
deafening. Every two days, the count came for news. Martin
scrupulously followed his master's orders for a long time, only
giving the white horse a handful of hay each day. But when the
handsome animal started growing so thin that his ribs could be

counted, he took pity on the noble beast. He began thinking, "If only I could feed him suitably." However, his intransigent master's order forbidding this returned to his mind ceaselessly and stayed his hand. The horse got so weak he could barely stand. This touched the old valet, who had long found the entire matter quite strange. He said to himself: "What would happen if I fed him correctly?" Finally he put thought into action and gave the horse as much hay and oats as it could eat. Once his appetite was satisfied, the horse began to neigh in a friendly fashion and said,[27] "May God reward you. If you wish to be happy forever, feed me once more with as much as I can eat, then climb on my back and ride around the lake at the foot of the castle, until we are back where we started. The count is going to pursue us, mounted on his black charger that gallops like a demon. But that is of little account because, when you see that he is getting close to us and we will not be able to escape him, strike the ground with the whip that is hanging in the horsemen's room and we will be saved." Martin thought it strange that a horse could talk, and replied, "If all this is true, I will follow your instructions."

"It's true," replied the horse, "I swear to you by God and all the saints," and he raised his right leg as if swearing an oath.

"I'm going to think about it," replied the old valet.

"Reveal nothing of what I've told you to another living soul," the animal implored him, "otherwise we are lost!"

Martin left the stable thinking about what he should do. "I've never met a horse that can talk before," he said, half out loud. "It's curious. And why is the count so concerned with this animal? I'm going up to the horsemen's room to see if there's a whip there; I've never noticed one." He climbed the stairs, entered the main hall, and found a beautiful whip with a gold handle hanging beneath an old portrait. "By God, this is truly strange! This whip must have come here today, and yet no one but me is in the castle." The more he thought about it, the odder it seemed. He was gripped by an irresistible curiosity that soon swayed him to accede to the white horse's wishes.

The next day he fed him as much as he wanted, then mounted the horse and set off toward the lake. But they had barely arrived there when the count came galloping toward them on his horse that was black as pitch and spitting fire from its nostrils. The white horse quickened his pace so much that he was soon covered in foam, but the other quickly cornered him. Everything seemed to be lost! Martin then struck the ground with the whip and immediately a hillock rose up in front of the count. The count's mount soon found his way around it, and resumed its pursuit of the fugitives with even greater enthusiasm. Gradually it drew closer and closer. Martin used the whip again and another hill formed between them. This is how the white horse was able to get back safe and sound to the point where they had started from. As soon as they got there, his hide fell off, and a young and handsome knight appeared before Martin. He grabbed his hand and shook it, saying, "May God reward you for rescuing me! I will be grateful to you until the end of my life." Barely had he finished uttering these words when a dreadful commotion made itself heard. They looked around and saw the ground swallowing up the count and his mount. The black horse was the devil in flesh and bone,[28] and he had come to fetch the miser.

The young count returned to his castle, where he was now lord, and where a peaceful, happy future awaited him. He kept the loyal Martin by his side for a long time, and also gave him a large and prosperous farm of which he later become the sole owner.

Ignaz Vincenz & Josef Zingerle,
Kinder- und Hausmärchen aus Tirol
(Innsbruck: Heinrich Schwick, 1911), 268–73.

In contrast to other tales involving a magical escape, this story opens in a very original way by featuring the jealousy and hunger for power of a miserly nobleman who will not shrink from anything in order to satisfy his ambitions. The conclusion is strongly reminiscent of the tone set by the exempla *in which the demons assume the shapes of black horses (TU 1642). Tubach recorded, for example, the* exemplum *of a dying miser being tormented by riders on black horses (TU 1490b). The devil's mount is regularly a black charger (TU 1618; 1643).*

6. How a Shepherd Made a Fortune

Austria

One summer day, the sheep of a shepherd's flock scattered in the forest to escape the heat. After vainly racing to and fro trying to get his flock together, the enraged shepherd abandoned his sheep and set off beneath the foliage.

Being used to walking, the shepherd found himself sooner than expected at the gates of the capital city, which he had never seen before. With his mouth open, he stood in wonder like a cow in front of the new stable door. Among the people there he spotted a man dressed in blue pants and a white tunic. This outfit amazed him and he addressed the man next to him: "My friend, can you tell me what kind of man wears blue pants and a white tunic?"

"He's a soldier."

"A soldier—what's that?"

"A soldier makes his living by serving the king; he has to stand guard and go on campaigns," the city dweller told him.

"That would suit me just fine," said the shepherd. "Could I become a soldier?"

"You're in luck because the sovereign needs a lot of men in anticipation of war with the neighboring king."

After asking quite a few more questions, the shepherd made his way to the palace and enlisted. As of the next day, the new recruit paraded through the streets of the capital, proud of his new outfit.

As soon as he learned how to handle his rifle and turn left and right, his turn came to take night duty. This would ordinarily not have intimidated him, as he was no coward if, as a comrade had warned him, his life were not in jeopardy. In fact, he would have to stand guard from eleven to midnight at the Devil's Crag, the very hour when the Evil One haunted these premises, and he had already torn a good number of soldiers to pieces. In panic, the shepherd thought of ways he could escape this danger. While his fellow soldiers were having lunch at the barracks, our hero took to his heels and left the city as fast as he could. Once outside the city, he ran into an old man who asked him why he was in such a hurry. The shepherd, used to speaking frankly, told him what he was doing. "My son, you are committing an evil action by fleeing. Go back and resume your post; simply draw a circle around you with your consecrated bayonet.* If you follow my advice, nothing will happen to you." These words reassured the fugitive, who did an about-face and returned to the city.

Eleven o'clock had yet to strike when our soldier took up his post in front of the Devil's Crag. He was bravely waiting to see what would happen, as he had taken the old man's advice and drawn a circle around him for protection from the devil's claws and teeth. At eleven o'clock, the evil spirit rushed toward him, but when he reached the circle[29] he could go no farther. He howled in rage: "Get out of there, otherwise I will rip you to pieces!" The soldier remained impassive and didn't move a muscle. The devil howled two more times, but it was in vain. In resignation, he then said, "You are the first to resist me. I'm going to reward you— follow me!" After thinking about it, the soldier obeyed. The devil quickly made his way to a certain spot in the crag, which he struck

---

*It was customary to consecrate sharp weapons.

with a gold rod, opening it at once. They went in, and the devil showed the stupefied soldier large quantities of gold, silver, and pearls.[30] When it came time to part, the devil gave the shepherd three magical objects,[31] telling him: "If you need money, come to the crag, strike it with the golden rod I'm giving you, and it will open. You can take as much treasure as you need. The vial contains a liquid: if you moisten locks with it, they will open.[32] Lastly, here is this black plant: place it on a pile of money and it will instantly separate the money earned honestly from that which was acquired dishonestly."[33] The devil then vanished.

The soldier wished to resume his post, but another guard was already there. He went to find his superior officer and told him what had happened. Because he could now get money without any trouble, he left the army and led a pleasant life, although he did not neglect the poor.[34] This is why he gave his impoverished cobbler a ducat every time he cleaned his boots. The poor shoemaker praised his benefactor for his great generosity. One morning, when the cobbler brought back his boots, the wealthy shepherd said, "I've already given you a lot, but it's too little. I'm going to make you a rich man. Come to my house this evening after dark." Wild with joy, the man left his benefactor and had nothing better to do than to trumpet the happiness awaiting him before everyone whose paths he crossed. The news traveled quickly by word of mouth until it reached the ears of the king. He summoned the cobbler, and after questioning him said, "I, too, am going to make you rich, if you lend me your clothes and you let me go to the shepherd in your place." The shoemaker agreed and promised not to reveal this subterfuge to anyone.

At nightfall, wearing the shoemaker's clothing,[35] the sovereign went to the shepherd's house. The man was already waiting for him and did not recognize him in the gloom. They then went to the house of a merchant suspected of deceit and usury. Moistened with the wondrous liquid, all the locks flew open and they reached the money chest. Once it was open, the shepherd set the black plant on the money and, lo and behold, immediately half the money, all that had been acquired dishonestly, jumped out of the chest. The king grabbed it, because the shepherd told him, "Take as much as you can!"

When they left the merchant's house, the monarch asked, "And if we went to the room of the royal treasury?"

"Don't you have enough already? Still you want more?" the shepherd replied. "I've never gone there and will not go today."

But the king kept insisting until the shepherd finally yielded. Once they were both in the treasury, the shepherd placed the black plant on the money pile. Nothing budged. The king waited for the shepherd to give him the order to take the money, but the shepherd remained silent. When the monarch plunged his hand into the pile of gold to take a few coins, the shepherd, horrified by this brazenness, told him, "Stop at once or I will break your arm in two. You should note well that I only take money that has been earned dishonestly!" They then left the room, and when they parted outside, the shepherd told the alleged cobbler, "You are poor and I wanted to make you rich, but as soon as you saw the gleam of gold, you revealed all your greed to me. Go away and don't expect any more help from me!"

The next day, the king summoned the shepherd and congratulated him for his integrity after revealing the secret of the previous night, and urged him to continue his charitable works. The shepherd heeded his request, thereby ensuring his own happiness as well as that of many others. On his deathbed, he left the three magical objects to the monarch.

THEODOR VERNALEKEN, *KINDER-UND HAUSMÄRCHEN AUS ÖSTERREICH* (VIENNA: BRAUMILLER 1863), 87–92.

ATU 314 A.

7. The Devil's Valet

Romania

A man went to a fountain, gazed into it, and shouted, "Come, come, come!" Immediately, a man with red eyes appeared and asked if he had a son that could serve him. "I have one," the man replied. "What kind of salary will you give him?

"One hundred florins."

"Fine. Where do I have to bring him?"

"Here."

When he came with his son, the devil told him: "Return here in one year; I will bring your son and the money." Then he dove into the fountain with his young valet.

At the end of the year, the father returned to the fountain and shouted: "Come, come, come!" The devil immediately appeared with the boy and the hundred florins and asked him if he couldn't leave his son for another year, and this time he would give him two hundred florins.

The boy had grown a lot bigger and stronger; he was almost unrecognizable, and his father left him with the devil.

When the second year ended, the father again returned to the fountain and shouted: "Come, come, come!" The devil appeared with the boy, but asked him if he didn't want to leave him for another year in return for three hundred florins, and the father accepted. When this year was up, the devil appeared and said, "I'm going to bring three boys; if you can't pick your son from among them, he belongs to me and I won't return him." The father feared he would make the wrong choice. Suddenly a bumblebee flew over to him that said, "When the devil brings the three boys, one of them will take out his handkerchief to catch me. That one will be your son."

When the devil arrived with the three boys, who were as alike as three peas in a pod, the bumblebee appeared, buzzing loudly. When one of the three boys pulled out his handkerchief to capture it, his father placed his hand on his shoulder and said, "This is my son." Having nothing to say in reply, the devil vanished. In three years his valet had picked up a lot of tricks.

One day when a fair was being held in their village, the son said to his father, "Let's go there to make some money! I will change into a stallion, and you will sell me for a good price to whoever wants to buy me—except for the man with red eyes." Once they were at the fair, a red-eyed man was already there, but the father told him, "I won't do business with you." Time passed, and then another red-eyed man came up. Thinking that no other buyer would come, the old man sold him the stallion. When the red-eyed man tried to slip a bridle on him, the horse transformed into a hare and started racing away, quick, quick, quick, with the devil hot on his heels. When he was just about to be caught, he changed into a crow and flew off, quick, quick, quick, with the devil in hot pursuit. Once again, when he was on the verge of being captured, the crow turned into a fish and sped through the water, quick, quick, quick, with the devil chasing him. Going to the bank, the devil asked a fisherman, "Have you seen an unusual fish around here?"

"Yes, yes, he's got a good seven hours head start on you."

The devil resumed his chase, and when he had almost caught up to him, the fish changed into a rooster that flew, quick, quick, quick, to the palace walls. He let rip a melodious cock-a-doodle-doo, the king's daughter came out, and with the devil right behind him, the rooster transformed into a ring that slipped, quick, quick, quick, right onto her finger. He advised her to not give the ring to anyone, no matter what they offered in exchange, and if her father tried to force her to give it up, she should throw the ring down on the ground and trample it underfoot until it was powder.

The devil sought out the king so he could ask to buy the ring.

The king ordered his daughter to give it to him, but she took it off her finger, threw it on the ground, stepped on it repeatedly, and ground it into powder. The powder produced millet, and the devil transformed into a rooster and started pecking at the grains, but he could not stop one of them from turning into a boy. The boy pulled out his knife and slit the rooster's throat. That's how he got rid of the devil.

He then married the princess and returned home to his father, who rejoiced to see him safe and sound. "See, Father, you almost caused my total ruin by selling me to a man with red eyes, but in the end you are responsible for creating my happiness."

PAULINE SCHULLERUS, *RUMÄNISCHE VOLKSMÄRCHEN AUS DEM MITTLEREN HARBACHTAL* (BUCHAREST: KRITERION, 1977), 234–36.

Bechstein 26, 51; Sklarek 25; Karadzic 6; Schullerus 25; Haltrich 14; Schott 19; KHM 68; Straparola VIII, 4.

ATU 325.

8. The Innkeeper

Italian Tyrol

He had a superb house and a beautiful field—the innkeeper of excellent reputation had long lived there, though we don't know exactly where it is. But the good man had an oversensitive heart and couldn't stand to see a poor person suffering from hunger or thirst. He would always prefer to give away his last piece of bread and last drop of wine. So it happened that not only did he not have any bread or wine for himself, but he was so buried in debt that his creditors wanted to sell his house and chase him out of it. Not a single person whom he had helped came to offer him aid or consolation. On the other hand, a man came in whom the innkeeper couldn't have tolerated during his glory days, "The proprietor will now give me a warm welcome," this man thought, "and won't reject me anymore, because he has learned better." This was the devil, and he offered this proposition to the innkeeper: "I'm going to lend you money for seven years, because your misfortune grieves me and you truly don't deserve it. But at the end of the seven years you have to pay me back in full. If you aren't able to, or if you are even a penny short, your soul will belong to me." The innkeeper knew full well whom he was dealing with but thought: "His conditions are completely reasonable. I could not only pay back the devil but all my creditors, and then I will be thrifty after that." He nodded and the devil gave him a huge sack of money that he used to pay off his debts. Laughing off his creditors, the innkeeper paid them back and enhanced the luster of his establishment, but he soon fell back into his old ways; incapable of ignoring the urges of his compassionate heart, he offered support to all the poor and his situation grew worse. One day, when the seven years were almost up, he was sitting sadly in front of his house. "Is it fair that my heart will belong to the devil," he thought to himself, "because I was too good?" Ruminating morosely like this, he didn't notice the arrival of three impoverished travelers until they were right in front of him, asking for alms. "I would gladly give you some money, and food and drink," he replied to their request, "but I don't have even a penny left to my name." It so happens that these three travelers were none other than Our Lord, Saint Peter, and Saint John. "You are a valiant man," Our Lord told him. "Ask me for three favors."

"Here are my three wishes: there is a fig tree over there and I want it so that anyone who climbs it cannot come back down against my will. I would also like that anyone who sits in the sofa in the main room cannot get up from it without my permission, and I would finally like that anyone who sticks his hands in the cashbox that's in the corner of this room cannot pull them back out if I don't permit it."

"I grant these wishes to you," Our Lord replied. "Always be good and charitable and everything will go well for you."

"L'OSTE DAI CUCCAI," IN CHRISTIAN SCHNELLER,
MÄRCHEN UND SAGEN AUS WÄLSCH-TIROL. EIN BEITRAG
ZUR DEUTSCHEN SAGENKUNDE (INNSBRUCK: WAGNER'SCHE
UNIVERSITÄTS-BUCH- HANDLUNG, 1867), 31–35.

📖 Shullerus 31; Asbjørnsen & Moe 23.

ATU 330 A, EM 12, COL. 111–120, MLEX 1033–1036.

This tale seems incomplete because the devil doesn't return to claim his due and the wishes are not used, contrary to the other stories providing the same structure.

TALE TYPES
IN THIS BOOK

*Based on the International
Classification of Antti Aarne
and Stith Thompson*

The examples in this concordance follow the classification system developed by Antti Aarne and Stith Thompson, as presented in their reference work *The Types of the Folktale: A Classification and a Bibliography*. The columns to the left give the number and name of the tale type, while the column on the right lists the stories in this collection that feature it, cited by chapter (Roman numeral) and section number (Arabic numeral). Asterisks are used in the classification system to further differentiate tale types.

APPENDIX 2

INDEX OF MOTIFS ASSOCIATED WITH THE DEVIL

This index is based on American folklorist Stith Thompson's *Motif-Index of Folk-Literature,* a six-volume catalog. A "motif" is a term used by folklorists to describe individual details within a tale. A motif may refer to a character, action, setting, or object. The examples of motifs found in Thompson's catalog and included in this appendix are organized by a motif number and a descriptor, defined as follows:

- The **motif number** is a letter and a series of numbers that are a shorthand way of referring to specific details found in folktales.
- The **descriptor** is a short verbal explanation of what each motif is about.
- The column on the right indicates the tale(s) in this collection featuring the motif—identifed by chapter (Roman numeral) and section number (Arabic numeral).

D 812.3.   Magical object received from the devil   VII, 6

F 81.2.	Journey to hell to recover devil's contract	V, 3
G 303.1.5.	Devil has tail	VI, 2
G 303.16.19.4.	Devil (Satan) flees when cock is made to crow	VI, 2
G 303.16.2.3.3.	Devils disappear when priest blesses bread	VI, 2
G 303.4.1.6.	The devil has horns	VI, 2
G 303.3.1.2.	The devil as well-dressed gentleman	I, 5
G 303.3.3.1.3.	The devil as horse	VII, 5
G 303.3.3.3.1.	Devil in form of raven	III, 2
G 303.9.1.	The devil as builder	I, 3
H 1131.2.	Devil as suitor assigned task to build bridge or dam	I, 3
H 1273.1.	Quest to devil in hell for return of contract	V, 3
H 523.	Test: guessing nature of devil's possessions	III, 11
J 172.	Account of punishments prepared in hell bringing about Repentance	V, 3
K 2325.	Devil frightened by threatening to bring mother-in-law	II, 2
M 210.	Bargain with the devil	IV, 2
S 211.	Child sold (promised) to devil	VII, 3

NOTES

INTRODUCTION

1. Fischer, *Das Buch vom aberglauben* (Leipzig: Schwicker, 1790), 2.
2. J. G. von Hahn, *Griechische und albanesische märchen,* 1st part (Leipzig: Wilhelm Engelmann, 1864), n 106. See the tale (story 2 in chapter 1 of this anthology), in which the motif of the chain reappears.
3. Johann-Joseph von Görres, *Die Christliche Mystik* VI, 14 (Landshut, 1836–1842).

CHAPTER I
THE DEVIL AS SUITOR

1. Variant of Motif N 211.1. Lost ring found in a fish.
2. Motif C 611. Forbidden chamber. Person allowed to enter all chambers of house except one.
3. Motifs R 157.1. Youngest sister rescues elder; E0. Resuscitation.
4. Cf. August Wünsche, *Der sagenkreis vom geprellten teufel* (Leipzig & Vienna: Akademischer Verlag, 1905), 83.
5. Motif H 1131.2. Devil as suitor assigned task to build bridge or dam.
6. Motif G 303.9.1. The devil as a builder.
7. Motif D 231. Transformation: man to stone.
8. Motif G 303.3.1.2. The devil as a well-dressed gentleman.
9. Motif C 611. Forbidden chamber. Person allowed to enter all chambers of house except one.

10. Motif Q 341. Curiosity punished.
11. Evald Tang Kristensen, *La Cendrouse et autres contes du Jutland,* trans. Jean Renaud (Paris: J. Corti, 1999), collection merveilleux, 9.

CHAPTER II
THE DEVIL AND HIS FAMILY

1. Motif F 641.3. Man can hear one sleeping by putting ear to ground.
2. Motif F 601. Extraordinary companions. A group of men with extraordinary powers travel together.
3. Motif K 2325. Devil frightened by threatening to bring mother-in-law.
4. Caballero, Fernán, *Obras Completas de Fernán Caballero.*

CHAPTER III
THE SWINDLED AND BATTERED DEVIL

1. Motif G 303.3.3.3.1. Devil in form of raven.
2. Motif N 451.1. Secrets of animals (demons) accidentally overheard from tree.
3. Motif H 523. Test: guessing nature of devil's possessions.
4. Motif H 543. Escape from devil by answering his riddles.
5. J. Árnason, *Íslenzkar þjóðsögur og aevintýri,* (Leipzig, 1862–1864), vol. 1, 485 *ff.*
6. Motif D 1412.1. Magic bag draws person into it.

CHAPTER IV
IN THE DEVIL'S SERVICE

1. Variant of Motif G 303.3.1.6. The devil as the black man.
2. This tale replaces the magician with the devil, which is a variant of: Motif D 1711.0.1. Magician's apprentice.
3. Motif D 100. Transformation: man to animal.
4. Motif C 837. Taboo: loosing bridle in selling man transformed to horse.
5. Motif K 252. Selling oneself and escaping.
6. Motif D 610. Repeated transformation. Transformation into one form after another.

7. Motif M 210. Bargain with the devil.

8. Motif Q 42.1. Spendthrift knight. Divides his last penny. He is later helped by the grateful person.

9. Motif D 1653.1.7. Infallible gun; Motif N 826. Help from beggar.

10. Motif D 1415.2.5. Magic fiddle causes dancing.

11. Motif D 1412.1. Magic bag draws person into it. This sack can also be seen in August Ey, *Harzmärchenbuch,* (Stade: F. Steudel, 1862), 118 *ff*.: the hero, a smith, captures three devils.

12. Motif N 55.1. Loser of shooting wager to go naked into thorns for bird.

13. Motif T 721.5. Subterranean castle.

14. Motif C 611. Forbidden chamber. Person allowed to enter all chambers except one.

15. Variant of Motif C 913. Bloody key as sign of disobedience.

16. Motif R 157.1. Youngest sister rescues elder.

17. Motif G 561. Ogre tricked into carrying his prisoners home in bag on his own back.

18. Motif F 771.4.3. Abandoned castle. Has no inhabitants when hero enters.

19. Motif B 211.1.3. Speaking horse.

20. Motif D 672. Obstacle flight. Fugitives throw objects behind them which magically become obstacles in pursuer's path.

21. Motif B 41.2. Flying horse.

22. Variant of Motif H 56. Recognition by wound; Motif H 86.4. Handkerchief with name on it.

23. Motif D 300. Transformation: Animal to person.

CHAPTER V
A VISIT TO HELL

1. Motif F 81.2. Journey to hell to recover devil's contract; Motif H 1273.1. Quest to devil in hell for return of contract.

2. Motif F 971.1. Dry rod blossoms. Cf. ATU 756: The hard penance and the green twigs on the dry branch.

3. Motif J 172. Account of punishments prepared in hell brings about repentance.

4. Variant of Motif D 215.5. Transformation: man to apple tree.

CHAPTER VI
THE DEVIL AND THE CHURCH

1. Motif D 1192. Magic purse.
2. Motif D 1163. Magic mirror.
3. Motif D 950.5. Magic pear tree.
4. Motif G 303.1.5. Devil has tail.
5. Motif G 303.4.1.6. Devil has horns.
6. Motif G 303.16.19.4. Devil (Satan) flees when cock is made to crow.
7. Variant of Motif G 303.16.2.3.3. Devil disappears when priest blesses bread.

CHAPTER VII
SINGULAR TALES

1. Motif D 1533.1.1. Magic land and water ship.
2. Motif D 1375.1.1. Magic fruit causes horns to grow on person. This motif plays a large role in the story of Fortunatus.
3. Motif D 1375.2. Magic object (fruit, nut, water, flowers) removes horns from person.
4. Variant of Motif F 350. Theft from fairies.
5. Motif K 1111. Dupe puts hand (paws) into cleft of tree (wedge, vise).
6. Motif Q 212. Theft punished.
7. Motif H 1400. Fear test.
8. Motif K 2320. Deception by frightening.
9. Motif S 211. Child sold (promised) to devil.
10. Motif N 836.1. King adopts hero.
11. The motif of nights of torture: D 758.1. Disenchantment by three nights' silence under punishment. This can be found in tale types ATU 326, 400 A, and 402.
12. Motif D 701. Gradual disenchantment.
13. Motif S 139.2. Slain person dismembered.
14. Motif E 30. Resuscitation by arrangement of members. Parts of a dismembered corpse are brought together and resuscitation follows.
15. Motif D 1470.1.15. Magic wishing ring.
16. Variant of the Motif C 932. Loss of wife for breaking taboo.
17. Motif N 843. Hermit as helper.

18. Motif D 1521.1. Seven-league boots.

19. Motif D 1067.1. Magic hat.

20. Motif D 1361.14. Magic cap renders invisible.

21. Motif D 1254. Magic staff.

22. Motif T 92.10. Rival killed.

23. Motif D 131. Transformation: man to horse.

24. Motif E 402.1.5. Invisible ghost makes rapping or knocking noise.

25. Motif E 402. Mysterious ghost-like noises heard.

26. Motif E 402.1. Noises caused by ghost of person.

27. Motif B 211.1.3. Speaking horse.

28. Motif G 303.3.3.1.3. Devil as horse.

29. Motif D 1272. Magic circle.

30. Motif N 512. Treasure in underground chamber (cavern).

31. Motif D 812.3. Magic object received from devil.

32. Motif D 1242.1. Magic water.

33. Motif D 965. Magic plant.

34. Motif W 11. Generosity.

35. Motif K 1816.10. Disguise as cobbler (shoemaker).

BIBLIOGRAPHY

Aarne, Antti, and Stith Thompson. *The Types of the Folktale.* Helsinki: Academia Scientium Fennica, 1961.

Asbjørnsen P. C. and Moe Jørgen. *Norske Folkeeventyr.* Christiania: J. Dahl, 1852. French translation: *Contes de Norvège,* 2 vol. Géménos: Esprit Ouvert, 1995–1998. English translation: *The Complete and Original Norwegian Folktales of Asbjørnsen and Moe.* Translated by Tiina Nunnaly. Minneapolis: Univ. of Minnesota Press, 2019.

Bechstein, Ludwig. *Le livre des contes.* Presented, translated, and annotated by Claude and Corinne Lecouteux. Paris: J. Corti, 2010.

Bolte, Johannes, and Georg Polivka. *Anmerkungen zu den Kinder- und Hausmärchen.* 5 vols. Leipzig: Dieterich/Welcher, 1913-1918.

Caballero, Fernán, *Obras Completas de Fernán Caballero. Cuentos y poesías populares andaluces,* Alicante: Biblioteca Virtual Miguel de Cervantes, (1916) 2017.

Cortes Vazquez, Luis. *Cuentos populares salamantinos II: De encantamiento, de animales,* Salamanca: Librería Cervantes, 1979.

Delarue, Paul, and Marie-Louise Ténèze. *Le Conte populaire francais,* catalog raisonné, volume 1. Paris: Erasmus, 1957.

———. *Le Conte populaire francais,* catalog raisonné, volume 2. Paris: Maisonneuve et Larose, 1964.

Espinosa, Aurelio. *Cuentos populares de Castilla y León.* Madrid: CSIC, 1987.

Gonzenbach, Laura. *Peppe le sagace, et autres contes siciliens.* Translated and annotated by Claude and Corinne Lecouteux. Paris: Imago, 2019.

Greive, Arthur, and Taloş Ion (ed.). *Brancaflôr. Märchen aus der Romania.* Preface by Rolf W. Brednich. Aix-la-Chapelle, 2009.

Grimm, Jacob & Wilhelm. *Contes pour les Enfants et la maison,* 2 vol. French trans. by Natacha Rimasson-Fertin. Paris: J. Corti, 2009.

Hahn, Johann Georg von. *Griechische und albanesische märchen,* 1er Teil. Leipzig: Wilhelm Engelmann, 1864.

Haltrich, Josef. *Deutsche Volksmärchen aus dem Sachsenlande in Siebenbürgen.* Berlin: Springer (Jacob Grimm), 1856.

Karadzic Stefanovic, Vuk. *Volksmärchen der Serben.* Berlin: Reimer, 1854.

Leskien, August. *Balkanmärchen.* Iéna: Eugen Diederichs, 1915.

Leskien, August, and K. Brugman. *Litauische Volkslieder und Märchen.* Straßburg: Trübner, 1882.

Obert, Franz. *Le Zmeu dupé et autres contes transylvaniens.* Transation, notes, and commentary by C. & C. Lecouteux. Paris: J. Corti, 2012.

Papahagi, Pericle. *Basme aromâne.* Bucharest: Rasidescu, 1905.

Ranke, Kurt et al (eds.). *Enzyklopädie des Märchens.* 11 vols. Berlin and New York: De Gruyter: 1979-2006.

Schott, Arthur & Albert. *Rumänische Volkserzählungen aus dem Banat.* Edited by Rolf W. Brednich and Ion Taloş. Bucharest: Kriterion, 1975.

Schullerus, Pauline. *Rumänische Volksmärchen aus dem mittleren Harbachtal.* Hermannstadt, 1907 (Archiv des Vereins für siebenbürgische Landeskunde, 33); in appendix: *Rumänische Volksmärchen aus dem Alttal.*

Sklarek, Elisabet. *Ungarische Volksmärchen.* Leipzig: Dieterich, 1901.

Staufe, Ludwig Adolf. *Basme populare din Bucovina,* O colecţie inedită. Edited by Viorica Nişcov and Helga Stein. Bucharest: Editura Saeculum, 2012.

Thompson, Stith. *Motif-Index of Folk-Literature.* 6 vols. Copenhagen: Rosenkilde and Bagger, 1955-1958.

Tubach, Frederic C. *Index exemplorum: A Handbook of Medieval Religious Tales.* Helsinki: Suomalainen Tiedeakatemia, 1969.

Widter, Georg, and Adam Wolf. "Volksmärchen aus Venetien." *Jahrbuch für Romanische und Englische literatur* 8 (1866): 3 *ff.,* 290–91, 382–84.

Zingerle, Ignaz & Joseph. *Les Plumes du dragon, contes des deux Tyrols.* Presented, translated, and annotated by Claude and Corinne Lecouteux. Paris: J. Corti, 2018.

INDEX